CALL SIGN CHARLEY ONE

"A true crime memoir"

By

MALCOLM CAMPBELL

Special Thanks:

I would like to take this opportunity to thank my ex-wife Donna Campbell for putting up with me through this challenging journey. I would also like to thank my children, Joshua, Jacob, Phoebe, Willow, and Roman, who are indeed a gift from the gods and fill my heart with love. Special recognition to my very dear friend Jim Ray, for without whom this true crime story would never have been told, and chances are, I would just be an etching on a gravestone if not for his frank advice and dear friendship.

I would like to thank Steve Brown for being that voice in my head, saying, "Campbell, just get it done." Special thanks to Mandy Brown, who was always my light guiding me out of the dark.

To all my dear friends for their support, especially those from Clee Hill and Cleobury Mortimer. Amie and Alex, Lou and Keelan, Lucy, and Deb. Thanks to Martyn, Julie, and family for your endless kindness and boundless enthusiasm. To Paul and Sue Elwood, for your friendship, I value so dearly. Richard and Maria Cook, two people I admire the most for their kind and loving nature and service in the police force.

To Joann Bailey, author, and warrior of life, who continues to astonish me daily, how kind, caring, and wonderful one can strive to be xx.

The Early Years

Slowly becoming conscious with one, then two eyes opening, I realized the blurred vision, and the stinging feeling in my eyes was surprisingly my blood. A stillness had engulfed my body as I lay in the nettles that surrounded me, daring not to move for fear of the thousand needle deaths that appeared inevitable. The night's darkness gave sight to the fact that I had been lying here sometime, as I never did see the night so dark, apart from inside my eyelids, while I snuggled a stuffed bear.

I contemplated as the pain started to awaken in my body, why me? Why are their people who do these things? I knew the beatings for that night were not over, as the darkness spoke to me that I should have been home way before the velvet veil of the underworld had caressed my being, and thus, I would have to face my father when I got home. Maybe, I thought? It was best to stay here. The rising of my chest appeared to slow, and my eyes flickered as the outside world started to fade.

I felt numb with the cold, and my wet clothes amplified this feeling. I could remember only one thing at that point as my thoughts drifted into a half-sleep state, the memory of my mom's perfume invoking my senses and wrapping around me like an invisible fur coat hug of love, which had cocooned my soul.

I prayed to God that someone would find me and take my eight-year-old fragile battered body back to my mother's embrace. My tongue felt swollen, and my lungs' vapour trickled into the night like an emptying bottle of magic potion. Sadness became my aura as I couldn't hear any footsteps on the gravel path beside me. It was a helpless realization. Unfortunately, what was more sinister is that this trauma was becoming a regular part of my life. It seemed God had plans for me that night, as I would not die that day.

I lived on a minor's estate as we had moved down from Scotland so my father could work in the coal mines, and my mother was a nurse. No matter what age I was, anytime you went out to play, someone stole off you or beat you up. Children would pretend to be your friend and take you somewhere obscure and turn on you, leaving you helpless, afraid, and alone.

I remember one summer when I didn't go out at all, just stayed in my bedroom most of the time. My two sisters, brother, and I, were raised as Roman Catholics, which seemed to mean it was okay to hit your kids with belts, as I witnessed and heard many times.

As a small boy my only memory was walking to school and back with my guitar singing Elvis songs where old ladies sometimes would wait at their gate to hear me as I worked past. I'm sure I wasn't that good! Although to stop me from getting into trouble, I do remember being put in the school choir and ending up having a voice as an angel culminating in auditioning to sing solo at Lichfield Cathedral live on TV. Once my voice broke, my singing career was over as quick as it started.

To say my childhood was a violent experience is an understatement. At secondary school, they called me SAM, a nickname standing for Sick and Mental. It wasn't that I had been born this way, only the years of beatings from kids on my estate and at school had tainted my soul, and over time, I had turned from this cute innocent cheeky boy to a walking bundle of hate and horridness.

I can recall my first day at school, running downstairs into my mother's arms, with my very posh brand-new uniform, which included an expensive blazer with the school logo and a brilliant brown leather soft briefcase. After breakfast, my mother waved goodbye for my two-mile walk through the concrete estate peppered with school children wearing fourteen-hole doctor martin boots, shaven heads, and smoking like a steam train.

Looking back at this time, it was no surprise that I came home that day with cuts and bruises, torn trousers, missing my blazer and satchel. Suffering an attack from boys on my estate, they had posted my bag and blazer into the post box. I was in deep trouble at home that day too. I used to struggle to understand why walking past someone was license enough to come over to you and smack your face in, followed by kicking me half-unconscious.

Why? I used to say. Why? What have I done to you? It made no difference; that's just how life was on this estate. I could detail the horrific beatings and horrible torture I endured, but seriously, why make you run to the toilet to throw up, but I think I must paint a picture.

I received torture of chicken wire tightened and wrapped around my head. Held down and shot at with air rifles. Pinned down with fireworks exploding in my coat. Stripped naked and humiliated, beaten unconscious with a house brick, poisoned, slashed, pissed on, drugged, assaulted well-over three hundred times, and thrown in the canal. The list could go on all day. Just a sample of what I will speak about, so I am sure you get the picture. This went on for three or four years.

After many years of this, mostly every day, I transformed like a werewolf under a full moon, a switch had turned in my mind, and I finally had suffered enough. My spirit screamed no more!

What followed can only be described as if listening to an overweight grey-haired, ex thug telling stories of gangster-style hits in the middle of London propped up at the bar, wallowing over his sixth pint and talking of legend stories. The transformation was incredible; not only could I fight, but I had learned how to take a beating and still fight. I knew I was sick because the things I wanted to do to some people out of revenge were simply disgusting on every level. After that day, I hunted everyone down with a scent of a newborn vampire with horrific supernatural strength.

I would see them as prey, sometimes laying in secret for hours waiting for them to come home or picking them off from a group one at a time, each revenge in its own unique design, leaving the rest of the group always in fear before their reckoning. The sick thing was I enjoyed it; nothing gave me more of an adrenalin rush than extracting excruciating pain while breaking bones, marinated in the blood of my wrath. Oh, I was utterly another level!

Within one month, I had already built a reputation of being horrifically mental in my approach and what I would do to them. I would often spend fifteen minutes with them in a brutal way, inflicting pure terror and horror.

Remember that cute little boy at the beginning of this story?

It is disgusting, right? Yes, one hundred per cent agree, but that is what violence and sickening acts do to people. Violence breeds violence. I was a loving, kind boy who loved to sing Elvis songs and play kindly with children.

Environmental learned behaviour, I believe they call it.

When I was eleven, my father re-mortgaged the house we lived in and spent it all gambling on horses as usual. Inevitably, resulting in our house repossession, and we were all kicked out.

My father ran away somewhere; my eldest sister, Catharine, had left home when I was six, never to see again. My second sister Irene moved in with a bloke off another estate. My brother Colin moved to West Sussex to train as a jokey, and my mother struggled to bring me up on her own; thus, over a short period, I had lost my whole family.

Emotionally, I cannot tell you how devastating that was for an eleven-year-old boy! My mother would work as a nurse through the night, which was the only job she could get, and I would be home alone and told to go straight to bed. Of course, I was out all night up to no good and fighting.

By the age of eleven, I was knocking out twenty-five-year-old skinheads, successfully beating unconscious the hardest wannabe

Rocky Balboa skinhead on the estate. I was deemed the hardest in the school by year three and would fight with the hardest of other schools in a champions competition. I had six large tattoos on my arms from my hell's angel mate, and I was already sporting a shaven head and fourteen-hole doctor martins with red, white, and blue laces. Yes, I was a full-blown no holds barred psychopath! It was only a matter of time before I killed someone, and at the age of fourteen, I found myself in court on an attempted murder charge. But before you gasp, it wasn't my fault. It was an accident of kind; well, I did set him on fire.

However, I would like to explain: That day my mom had sent me to the shops to get some groceries, we had moved to another godforsaken area in my town that was even worse than the original place I grew up. As I walked towards the shop, I could see a boy coming down the path on his chopper bike past a school. He was a tall lad, probably around the age of seventeen, greasy hair, ugly twat. He stopped just in front of me, and as I tried to get around him, he punched me in the face. "Give me your fags" he shouted at me! As I opened my pockets to give him my eight Rothmans, while deciding exactly how I was going to torture him under the subway one night, he moved his bike forward slightly past me.

He wore a tight denim jacket with the copper style buttons and the threads hanging out the back. "Give me a light," he said: So, I thought, I will give you a f***g lite. Lighting a few of the threads at the back of his jacket, but they appeared to go out. "Next time I see you you're dead", he said: as he cycled off.

Holding my bloody nose, I continued to walk towards the shop when I heard a scream! He had fallen off his bike, the flames moved up inside his jacket and engulfed his hair! Now he was ultimately on fire! I ran back to him, but he was rolling around the grass, screaming, trying to put out the flames and was not too happy to see me. "You're a F****g psycho", he said, "you are going down for this." Meaning I was going to go to juvenile prison. Smiling as he struggled to walk, pushing his bike with his still smouldering clothes, "Not so F***g hard now are ya," I yelped.

Later that night, the CID kicked in my door and arrested me for attempted murder, but every action has a reaction, Right? If he had not assaulted me, I would not have done what I did. The courts found me guilty but not under attempted murder, more destruction of property, and misadventure. I got three years' probation and one hundred- and thirty-hours attendance centre to attend. The scheme was a centre that the government had designed to keep football hooligans away from matches, where attendance was every other Saturday for five hours at a time, which involved being beasted by ex-army Physical training officers in the gym. Round the fields and in the swimming pool. It was like day prison, which only did one thing, got me fitter, to run and fight better.

However, I will say, the worst thing about this process was when my mom had to take me on the first day. This ex-Soldier was screaming at my mother, telling her my behaviour and how I had turned out was her fault. She was crying so much, and I hated the Ba****d for it. It was the first time I had seen her cry. I usually only heard it from upstairs, while my father was shouting or slapping her about. Horrible to witness her crying, as it was not her fault. She had done her absolute best with me under the circumstances. It was the shit hole I was living in what was F***d up, not her method of raising me.

I swore to myself that I would not put her through any more pain after that first day, and I promised her that I would try to be a credit to society, rather than a burden. By then, people at school and on the streets had heard about my so-called attempted murder accusation, and they had all decided to stay away from me because I was unstable? Luckily for me, then it was all paper files, and any offence before you were sixteen got removed from your record.

Unfortunately, keeping my head down did not go too well; after I got accused of carrying a knife in school, they asked me to leave, not expelled, but more go or dismiss you. Learning of this, my wise mother could see that I might be heading for prison if I kept on this path, and I should go and live with my brother in Arundel, West Sussex, and thank God she did this.

My first day in Arundel, walking down the street, everyone was saying good morning to me and smiling. I was walking with my head slightly down with a rocky kind of swagger and expecting trouble any minute, and everyone was so lovely. It dawned on me very quickly that the world was not full of hatred and violence. It was just that hell hole I had been living in that had given me the impression that the world was like this.

Now, I had a choice, to be a kind and law-abiding young man, and fit in? Or continue being a dick head. From this day, I never got in trouble again. Oh, I had a few fights, but it was nearly always self-defence.

I started a job washing up in a cafe and was doing well until the owner popped out, and a customer came in and asked for a cream tea, so I made her a cup of tea and filled it up with squirty cream. I got sacked that day.

I started working in a bakery, and I loved it apart from the early morning starts, I was on the sweet table, making doughnuts and cakes. I had been there for about six months until this lad started on the bread section. He had ginger hair, he was skinny and very goby. For some reason, he instantly disliked me, laughing, and joking about me with all the other lads on the bread table. Building up over time, he shouted over to me that he was going to kick my head in after work!

"Oh, here we go", I thought, another F****g twat that thinks he's Rocky Balboa, so the day continued with his snide remarks and his bullying tone, everyone getting excited to see the fight after work. Just another excellent example of a bully picking on the quiet one, I thought. I was getting so upset that someone was going to hurt me, and for what? I had not said or done anything to him to make him hate me. My heart was racing, and my blood pressure was sky-high. I was disgusted; this person was going to force me to fight. "Oh, no, I thought." As I was more scared of what lay within me coming out than I was of this goby, streak of piss.

We all finished together and walked into the changing room to take off our bakers' uniform. I was very sombre, not saying a word. He was acting the big man, showing off his pre-fight speech, reiterating how he was going to stamp all over my face. My memory is a bit blurred on this point, but something happened. According to reports, he was savagely and brutally attacked just as he took his baker's trousers down. Knocked down instantly and kicked around the floor like a lifeless rag doll, whimpering and crying with every striking blow. I can't tell you any more details; that's all I know; it must have happened after I had left.

So, I thought it was time for a new job, and I started a career in a wimpy burger restaurant in Bognor Regis. Well, I wasn't there long either as the scouse head cook was another bully wanting to flex his muscles and make me the butt of his jokes, so I only lasted three days, after someone knocked him out with a fire extinguisher in full view of the restaurant. I was starting to get bored of the south coast. I was about eighteen by now, can't remember my birthday being anything special, or if I got anything for it, not that I was bothered, so I decided to move back to the hell hole to see and live with my mom.

I had been away for three or four years by then, and on arriving home, I got an instant job as a cook in a little chef, where I was thrilled because there were loads of pretty girls working there, and I fancied at least five of them.

I became good friends with a guy called Rob; he was a 26-year-old handsome guy but with a dark side. He was having an affair with one of the waitresses, who was only about eighteen years old. She was a slim girl with a lovely smile, short curly hair with green eyes, stunning and beautiful, but she would cry so much as he used her and went back to his wife. I got close to this girl, and she told me how much in love she was with him. So, I decided to romance her over time and eventually sleep with her, showing her that she was attractive and could have any nice guy if she so chose. After a couple of weeks, I finished with her, but it was long enough to see good with her own eyes now. She thanked me and decided to leave home and go to college. I was so happy for her, and I hope she had a beautiful life as this was thirty-one years ago. Of course, Rob found out and hated me after that, but I could hold my head high. I wasn't the one cheating on my wife and making a young girl's life a misery.

Enter waitress number two, "oh my" a beautiful girl called Sara. I'm sure she won't mind me talking to you about her. Sara was like the head girl at school, stunning, smart, and sexy. The girl everyone wanted to be like if you were a girl, of course. Why, oh, Why? She wanted to go out with me, I have no idea, I think she loved the bad boy, and I guess I was kind of that stereotype, so eventually, we got together.

She was terrific in every way, such a gift to spend my time with her, but it didn't last that long when I broke it off with her. I guess I thought she was too intelligent, beautiful, and smart for me and that it would never work, or that I was afraid she would get rid of me, so I did it first, I don't know…but I do have very fond memories of Sara.

Caroline Jenkins was crucial to my life. She was the cutest, prettiest girl I had ever seen with an adorable laugh and a smile that melted your heart. Her eyes casting a spell on me instantly as we made contact. My heart started pounding as she gave me a big smile holding out her hand. I remember her skin feeling warm, soft, and electric. I fell in love with her at first sight within seconds, and I knew she had to be mine, making a claim on her secretly to the rest of the workforce. We had two years together, and for one year, I believe she stayed a virgin as I respected her wishes so much and to be honest, although I wanted to spend time with her in that way, I felt blessed just to be in her company and to hold the position as her boyfriend. My life would change forever from Caroline's few words, as she made eye contact with me, touching my face with her angelic hands, and convincing me that I was talented enough to go to college and train as a chef. At first, I laughed and said, "who? Me?" But she believed in me more than my whole family, and as such, I decided I would go and apply.

To my astonishment, I got in due to my years of working in cafes and restaurants, although I didn't tell them what they didn't want to here.

I found that I was good at college and would volunteer my help after college to chef Mr Arundel. He was a very experienced and kind natured lecturer, and for a year or so after college lessons finished, I would go in and learn butchery. I guess my efforts were appreciated when I won an award for outstanding contribution to food preparation and cookery. Astonishing as I had never been congratulated for any academic work before!

Sadly, Caroline and I parted after I decided to go to Amsterdam for a weekend with my friend, and she didn't like it, telling me if I went, then that was it. I come back excited to see her only to hear she had got a new boyfriend. My first heartbreak, I felt like my insides had been ripped out, leaving a hot knife which turned every few moments. I was so upset, crying in the locker room. I swear, with all my heart, I could have married that girl! I hope her life turned out happy, safe, and fulfilling? I still miss her smile now, even after twenty-eight years.

I was getting to know other students on the course, and I made friends with many, including Ashea, Donna, and Pete, who all became great friends. We would go dancing in the local club at least twice a week. They were all cool; actually, I would later marry Donna in 1996.

While in college, I had a desire beyond most to be a great chef, and as such, I was able to complete the professional hospitality diploma in record time, leaving almost a full year left of my two-year course. After some negotiations, and having little choice, my college decided to bring in an advanced qualification, called the advanced diploma in culinary arts, based on Escoffier. It was a full and in-depth form of cookery, which five of us started, and three weeks later, I was the only one left.

Shortly into year two of college, my father died. I was at college and got a phone call while volunteering to help in the night restaurant as a stand-in head chef. I should have been home as he was coming to live with my sister, and I would see him that night for the first time in an extended period. I missed my chance to say goodbye, which still upsets me now. After some time off from college, I returned and finished the course.

Graduating with an advanced diploma in French cuisine, I went straight to the Grand Hotel in Brighton, where I shared accommodation with a guy called Drew. He was a beautiful, kind guy, and we occasionally hung out together. I later found out he was gay, not that it bothered me or that it should. I joked and said, "all this time, I've been stripping off in front of you, and you didn't tell me." He laughed and said, "it's okay, sweetheart, you're not my type." I liked Drew, but felt oddly offended, and amusingly insulted I wasn't his type.

Two years later, I worked as a head chef for a restaurant in Staffordshire, and my girlfriend Donna joined me working as a restaurant manager. Unfortunately, our manager and owner were an alcoholic, and I couldn't see that our future was rosy. After a holiday in Sri Lanka for two weeks, lying on a beach, we decided that life was crap, and we needed to change things, so when we came back, we never went back and finished that job. Much to the dismay of the owner.

Flicking through a paper one day, I viewed an advertisement for a chef in the army. Then it clicked, I thought, my life isn't going in the direction I wanted, and the military could offer a stable job and security. So that was it, I started the application process. Attending selection in Lichfield barracks, ironically near the attendance centre, I had to go to many years before. I was beasted around the basic fitness test and just scrapped in by one second off the eleven-minute thirty seconds cut off time. The selection officer said my raged sprint at the end was the deciding vote to keep me.

Donna and I had set a date for our marriage, 06/07/96, we were delighted, passing all the army tests bringing this recruit closer to acceptance, and then we got my intake day. 07/07/96.

I would go from a three-piece suit to a shaven head and a boiler suit within twenty-four hours.

Our wedding was fabulous, and the family put great effort into making it that way. The next day, I was taken from our honeymoon suite to the railway station with my travel warrant for twelve weeks of army training at the home of the guards, Pirbright Regimental Training Centre. Waving goodbye to my new wife was emotional, and it sucked.

I fondly remember getting to Pirbright railway station and being met by an Army Corporal. "Welcome to Pirbright, may I take your bag, sir? Please get into the minivan, and I will escort you to the camp. "Oh, he is a nice guy, I thought." Then as soon as we arrived, and he opened the sliding door he shouted in the loudest voice. "Get out the f*****g van and stand to attention Campbell." "Oh, f**k", I thought, what have I done?

I recall with ease that every day was hell, and I called Donna most days, saying that I might be home the next day, as so many recruits were getting kicked out for one reason or another. There were recruits even escaping at night, climbing out the dorm window and jumping the fence. That gives you an idea of how tough it was.

I was 26 years old and very unfit. I hated anything to do with running, and we ran everywhere, even to the cafeteria. I loved the firing range and how smart we looked in our uniforms. I thought I was hard when I joined, but I was not.

After twelve weeks, they had broken me down to a quivering mess and built me up into a gentleman, who would die happily for our Queen and Country. After losing two stone in weight, I was sharp, conscientious, thoughtful, skilled, and a real trained badass. I felt so different, and I was immensely proud to be a soldier and make a positive contribution to our country.

I had sworn Allegiance to Her Majesty Queen Elizabeth, to protect those who cannot defend themselves and, from that day, I served with pride, narrowly missing out on the award of the best recruit. I was eventually posted to the helicopter regiment, the Army Air

Corps with 4 Regt in Wattisham Airfield, Ipswich, and Donna came and joined me in our marriage quarter.

I served for nine months in Africa and then ten months in America at Fort Lewis. I stayed serving for four years and participated in cookery competitions within the combined services. I was the only chef I come across within the Army that had specialized in Escoffier cuisine, which gave me an exceptional edge. I won two silver medals in the combined services culinary arts competitions and a silver medal best in class from the British Guild of Chefs. As I had mastered butchery in college, the Army used that knowledge by utilizing my skills in escape and evasion exercises, dropping me off in the middle of Dartmoor or Salisbury planes with maps, caged chickens, and a knife. I would then have to make myself shelter and conceal myself over the next five days while the Parachute regiment, the Gurkhas, and Marines, would find me on a map heading. I would train them to make an animal kill in the field, taking it down as fast as possible and without detection. Skinning, dissecting, and cooking without food poisoning themselves.

Kill, prepare, cook, sterilize, bury the remains, and move in record time. Watching Paras and Marines running around in the dark, trying to catch a chicken with its head cut off, is a memory I will always smile about. My staff sergeant was called Staff Little. He was a marathon runner, much to our platoon's delight, and would have us running or in the gym every day before we had to report for duty. It was doing it or get jailed. Two years later, I ran eighteen miles in wind and rain without stopping and continued to train for the London Marathon.

I had never been jailed or charged, which was miraculous, to be honest as it was common practice, even if you had not shaved brilliantly, you could get arrested. I guess I must mention that my mom died while I was away in the Army. It shook my world, she had always done her best by me, and I loved her dearly, she had a hard life, with not much happiness from what I could remember, and I didn't help much in that area, for that, I will always deeply regret not being a better son and not being there to say goodbye. She died from a stroke and remained still sitting up in bed with a book in her hands, so it would appear death was instant, for that I am grateful.

I served four years for the Royal Logistic Corps attached to 4 Regt Army Air Corps, which was a key player in 24 Airmobile Brigade. The whole experience gave value to my life as I had achieved what few were able to do and they made a gentleman out of me who would protect those that cannot defend themselves in the name of Queen and Country.

To what extreme, I would later find out would be my destiny.

Upon leaving the Army and starting up a catering business, I was enthusiastic and motivated. Donna and I were blessed with two sons, we called Joshua and Jacob and a daughter named Phoebe. All I wanted to do was cuddle them all the time, but long hours and pressures to be at work made it difficult to be the dad I wanted to be. The catering business went well for two years, but I worked ninety hours a week on my own for 12-15 hours a day until one day, I made a mistake.

I had turned on the gas in my mobile kitchen, and there was a leak. Being used to the smells of vapour's and such as a chef, I was not overly concerned. After fifteen minutes, I decided to light the equipment, and I was blown five feet into the air, completely engulfed in flames, rolling around the floor, trying to put myself out. Luckily for me, I had not opened a vent in the roof, so the explosion burnt through all the oxygen and the fire went out quickly. It was a bad day! I was rushed to A and E and quickly got liquid morphine, and then everything was my best day! My burns healed without scaring, and I was fortunate to be treated by such a professional team who took care of me promptly and with urgency.

After leaving the hospital, I spent four days in bed recovering and decided that was it with cooking. I decided that I would fall back on my army training and become a security officer. Most of the adverts were basic with low pay until I viewed one asking for the best ex-military personnel. My decision was clear, and that is what I was going to do.

They advertised themselves as the best in the country and the hardest to get in. I knew I had to join, and whatever came my way, it would be a snip compared to the hell training camp I had completed and the four years of military service. After several interviews, criminal checks, and medicals, I was shortlisted to attend their notorious training camp in the south near Guilford. My bags were packed with my train warrant in hand to attend my three-day residential training course.

The classroom was cold, with old school desks, school plastic and metal chairs, and a blackboard. It was a former Army training centre with accommodation from the sixties, with an oval tin roof and wooden window frames that whistled in the windy night. The ex-Paratrooper stood at the front, scanning us with his Sgt Major frown and his 3 Para tracksuit top, ready to bark at anyone who was not focused. I counted about twenty-five of us. All intrigued why this company was the best in the country.

"My name's Tom," said the ex, Para. "If you are scared to be stabbed, punched, or beaten to the floor, you can get up now and go back to your mummy." "I pondered for a moment and thought that sounds like home, giggling to myself." Silence fell over the class as we all looked at the guy next to us, to see if they would leave. The sound of squeaking chair legs started to echo around the room on the highly polished floor as one, two, then five guys stood up, and all said, we are going. Putting down their application forms, leaving, and that was it for them.

Twenty of us left, and we had no idea what was about to come in the next three days. One thing was for sure. We were all nervous and somewhat scared of the unknown. We did lots of fitness and martial arts on mats in the gym, which I enjoyed immensely as I had five belts in Karate and experience in Kung Fu.

My semi-contact karate training was perfect for the practical assessment as I successfully dropped three of my opponents in record time. Moving through to the final appraisal, of one against three, where honestly, I was sorry about the broken nose and the fractured knee, but they did come in hard.

Who would have guessed that only three of us would walk out of the gates with our train warrants and our confidential assignment?

First Assignment

"So, it's your job to keep the rats out!" "Just don't let them in, they're bloody everywhere," explained Mr Pleet, my new department store manager. Your call sign is Charley One, and the CCTV room is Delta Two; make sure you sign in and get to know the other store security guards as they will help you if you help them. We have a zero-tolerance here; if you catch them, I want them arrested and banned from the building.

Mr Pleet was about fifty years old, very charismatic, and smartly dressed, with grey hair and a stocky build, wearing a new grey pinstripe suit and shiny polished expensive shoes. After handing over my radio, office keys, and instructions, he swiftly walked off.

That was my introduction, now it was all on me to keep out the criminals.

Reaching for my radio and calling the CCTV room, I sent "Charley One calling Delta Two, are you there?" There was a bit of a chuckle, then a voice responded: "Delta Two, Delta Two to Charley One, receiving you loud and clear over." Pausing and a little unsure what to say, I sent back…" just signing in Delta Two." "Delta Two to Charley One, Yes, Yes, Received that over, Good morning Charley One."

Blimey, I thought, it's a bit scary talking into the radio when you don't know the correct format and words to say. About thirty minutes later, there was a security call over the store speaker: "Can security please come to door number four, please." Where's door four? I thought? As I approached a member of staff to ask, she kindly told me where to go. I hope it's not a shoplifter, I thought, I've only just walked through the door on my first day!

As I walked towards the desk in the department by door four, a lady from behind the counter says, "Hello, my name Anne." "This gentleman has come to see you." pointing to a tall 6ft 4 individual standing by the double glass door. Reaching out with his hand to shake mine, he said: "Hi, I'm Toby, I work in the CCTV room, and I've come to introduce myself." "Hi Toby, I'm Malc," as I shook his hand.

"Are you new," he said? "Yes, I am Toby, first day today." "Really," he said. "In for a culture shock, I am afraid, we have two homeless shelters on each side of the town, and we get hit by a constant stream of shoplifting from each side every day." "There are faces you need to learn quickly but do not worry, we usually have eyes on them before they get to the town." "You need to be incredibly careful of some of them, though, as he listed their code names, using radio speak." "Whiskey Kilo is a head case, don't even think about approaching him, stand back, and call Zulu Mike on the radio to go straight through to the police station." "Also, Papa Lemma, he's just been released from prison and is always a handful." Toby mentioned a few others, but my mind was too busy thinking what the hell have I got into. Is he blowing the situation out of proportion? Or speaking the truth? I thanked Toby, and he made his way out of the store.

I continued my rounds being a visual deterrent and making acquaintances with all the nice girls on the department desks. That day ends quickly, as I locked up my office and said goodnight to everyone at the door.

Arriving home, I recall my usual procedure, kissing my kids, catching up on their wellbeing, having some food, and going to the pub. Homelife was a bit awkward, we were growing apart, and I am sure I didn't help the situation heading off to the pub all the time. Donna was a truly kind natured lady and a great mom; she certainly deserved better, but we were having trouble, and I didn't feel there was an easy answer.

Three days into my new job and all was well, but things were about to change forever. I arrived in my smart uniform, polished combat boots, with a neat hairstyle. Setting up my new videotapes in my security office and doing the first rounds of the department store, everything seemed just a typical, easy day until I heard the call.

"Can Mrs Robinson report to the cosmetics department, please?" Echoing out of the internal store speaker. Shit! My heart started pounding, my legs went weak, and my arse was twitching, that's the code name for a theft in progress! Instantly, I was breathing heavy, the blood rushed to my face and hands as I could feel a mild panic starting to take place. Making my way quickly through the store, I arrived at cosmetics to see one of the supervisor girls point me in the direction of the double doors that lead to the side street. Getting on my radio, I called the CCTV room, sending: "Charley One to Delta Two, can you put the cameras on Walter street?" I believe I've got a theft in progress, stand by." "Delta Two to Charley One, Yes, Yes, cameras ready now."

As I slowly moved my head into a position that could see through the glass interior doors, I observed a white male with a screwdriver and a large bag, trying to unhinge the glass doors of a cabinet that held expensive bottles of aftershave and perfumes. The man was dirty, tall, and very gaunt-looking, with yellow-tinged skin. He looked rough and had that hard life look about himself. I stepped back to the radio once more: "Charley one to Delta Two attempted selection in progress, stand by." Just then, one of the girls came over to me and said he has just left.

Running to the cabinet, I could see he had given up trying to get the glass doors off and had entered Walter street. Sending instructions to the CCTV room that he had exited without concealment, I followed him outside and stood to see if I could get eyes on him. "Delta Two to Charley One, he's walking towards the town square, it's Whiskey Kilo." I paused and thought, I've heard that name before off Toby; what did he say about him again? I couldn't remember the details.

The town was busy with people shopping everywhere. I was trying to get eyes on Whiskey Kilo but couldn't see him anywhere. I walked up towards the square hugging the line of the shop windows to limit my detection, I heard the call, "Charley One from Delta Two, do you read me?" "Yes, go ahead, Delta Two" "He's turned and spotted you; he's coming right towards you." "Delta Two, where is he? I haven't located him yet."

"Delta Two to Charley One, he's picking up speed, stand down and go back into your store!" "Charley One to Delta Two, what direction, I still can't see him?" "Delta Two to Charley one, in 5......4.....3.......2......A horrendous pain shot through my head as

I was thrown against the plate glass window with this raging animal swearing and spitting in my face, grabbing me by my shirt, clumped into both his furious fists, he launched me almost off my feet into the view of his six-foot two stature. His eyes wear bulging with fury, and his face was tight and twitching as the anger exuded through every muscle in his face and jaw. Swearing profusely at me with his mouth almost touching mine, as he laid a barrage of abuse at me, with every word, spitting his vulgar mucous onto my face with my head continuously smashing against the window. It was like, everything you would imagine, but never experienced from an attack inside a prison.

I didn't know what to do, the radio was screaming "Charley One, Charley One." CCTV was calling an emergency response from Zulu Mike, the police. My head was being smashed harder against the window as he tried to knock me out, and I was utterly in shock. What could I do? How can I get out of this? I can't punch him. I'm on camera, I have no idea how to get out of this. I could feel my arse twitching with farts trickling out. "I can smell your fear" he screamed "Your nothing but a plastic copper, weak and pathetic." "Stay the f***k away from me, or next time I will f****g kill you."

Just then, a man came over and flashed his warrant card; it was an off duty police officer: "Let him go and piss off before I drag your arse into the cells," he said: Whiskey Kilo looked at me for a second with his eyes that screamed the fact he was dead inside, turned and walked away.

The police officer asked if I was okay? I thanked him and turned to go back to the store. By now, I looked like I had been run over by a truck, my shirt was hanging out, buttons ripped off, spit on my face while feeling my head to see if there was any blood. I was white as a sheet, as I looked at my reflection in the mirror in my office. My hands were shaking, and my mouth was dry; putting my hand over my mouth, trying desperately not to cry. Still shaking, I thought I would straighten myself up and go out the back ramp for a cigarette.

I certainly felt like I needed one.

Delta Two had called and asked me to ring the CCTV room. Toby asked if I wanted to press charges against Whiskey Kilo. I said no, it's okay, I will be fine, he never stole anything, and he never punched me he just slammed my body and head several times into the window and scared the living daylights out of me, which was worse than being hit.

That one single event of horridness seemed to destroy every piece of confidence I had in my body. Like an invisible virus that swallowed up my inner strength, I was terrified, scared, and genuinely felt something inside died that day. I was not someone who hurts or threatens people anymore, I was civilised and obeyed the law, I was a father and family man.

Going home, I couldn't tell my wife and admit that someone had done that to me, and I was helpless to react. I had just become an ordinary civilian who keeps out of trouble. I was like a pathetic bunny rabbit, and he was the rottweiler, picking me up and shaking me in his jaws, then dropping me out of disgust of how weak and fragile I was. Leaving me to live every day after that, in fear that he will come back, or that I might bump into him on my way to my car, without my store radio, so I could not call for help.

The days past and every day, I just felt like crying all day, every day. What was going on with my emotions? I could not tell anyone; I was too ashamed, too embarrassed. I would go home and just go straight to bed, telling my wife I felt sick. My kids wanted to play with me, but I could not clear the nightmare out of my mind. I felt so alone, so very profoundly alone and scared. I realised I had become a victim.

At work, I would hide in my office and pretend that I was busy, turning down the radio if other stores called for help from any available guards. Even direct calls to me asking for urgent help from stores just outside my door, I would turn off the radio and hide in my office. I felt pathetic, a loser, a coward. Very quickly, the staff was whispering and turning their heads, not communicating like they used to. I sensed they were disappointed in me, as I was not visual as much as I used to be. Chatting and smiling like the healthy person I was, and they were right. I feared I was just not capable of doing this job. I doubted my own ability, my confidence was gone.

It had seemed part of me had died, the part I liked so much about myself, my energy, my pleasantness, engaging with smiles and compliments, bringing happiness to others, and making them feel good about themselves which made me think I was a good member of the team. I missed the talks I used to have with everyone, especially the pretty girls, because they were a pleasure to talk to, and I wanted everyone to feel safe because I was there.

Now I couldn't look anyone in the eye, I walked mostly with my cap on and head down, hiding my fearful eyes from those that would look. I couldn't even look at myself in the mirror, I was so upset with myself that I had disappointed everyone.

At home, I stopped going out, I was depressed, withdrawn for almost two weeks after the incident, I was still going to bed really early, so I didn't have to have any personal contact with my wife, and so she couldn't guess there was something wrong with my silence. I just did not feel anything anymore apart from being nervous all the time, everywhere, even at home. If my children jumped on me on the couch, I would flinch back in fear.

From the time of the attack, it must have been four weeks later, and by now, it seemed everyone had lost confidence in my ability to act and work like a security officer. I would hear radio talk saying, they would call Charley One for help, but they know he won't leave his store now. I would see dodgy-looking criminals pointing and laughing at me through the window as I patrolled, obviously suggesting I was not up to the job.

One morning I was called to the side street by an internal call from the store to say that a customer needed urgent assistance. As I approached the door, I could see through the double glass doors that an elderly lady was lying on the tarmac. I walked through the door to help her up; She was a small lady about four foot, fragile and tiny. I had assumed she had fallen over, approaching her, and sending Delta Two a message to put the cameras on me while I assisted, I noticed blood on the pavement around her head. Kneeling, I observed she had been attacked.

She was in her mid to late eighties, with veins showing clear on her hands and a dark brown coat with white-grey hair. She was in terrible pain, crying and moaning as the pain shot through her body. Asking her to lay still, I sent to Delta Two that we needed an ambulance. Blood was coming out of her mouth, and her false teeth lay broken on the tarmac. Her white hair which was thin and matted now discolored with dark red blood. I held her in my arms, and a woman from a shop came running over to me and said she witnessed what had happened.

A young lad had punched her three times in the face while grabbing her handbag and making off towards the direction of Sainsbury's supermarket. The old ladies' cries and moans of pain were so horrible to observe, as I held her head in my arms, she was struggling to talk, as she started to choke on her own blood, and seemed to be unresponsive at times as I quickly put her in the recovery position.

I could hear the ambulance sirens coming closer, and I stayed with her until the paramedics arrived as Delta Two monitored the whole incident. I felt a moment like Deja Vous, where I thought I had seen and heard the sirens and blood before as if this was a calling home on some deep spiritual level.

I asked if the shop assistant could give me a description of the male, and helpfully, she did, which I relayed back to Delta Two, who said they would scan the area towards the river and Sainsburys.

Witnessing this frail old lady, having been brutally attacked for her handbag, ignited anger within me. It would make any respectable members of society feel the same disgust. An adrenaline rushing throughout my whole body started to build, fueling every ounce of muscle tissue with pure, undiluted fury. The swear words that were going through my mind about this individual who had done this were not repeatable. In that single moment, I forgot about my own attack and just wanted vengeance on every single despicable, cowardly, scum bag that prayed on innocent, vulnerable, law-abiding people.

Suddenly the soldier within was awakening, but so was that person I used to be, growling like a ravaged dog in a cage, snapping at the bars, ferocious and demonic, out of his dark limbo where I had suppressed him for so many years.

My one thought at that moment in time, I will never forget as I no longer felt fear. I felt a despicable level of disgustingness towards these criminals. Now I almost felt sorry for them in a sick twisted knowledgeable way. As at that moment, I looked down at that poor defenceless lady, so fragile and weak being treated by the paramedic, and in my mind, I declared my own personal f****g war against the whole f****g lot of them.

I could feel the tensing of my face, the gritting of my teeth, and the blood swelling in my shoulders and neck; my breathing became shallow but fast, and I was ready for a massive fight.

I washed this ladies' blood off my hands in the store's toilets, and as I did, I looked into the mirror and into my own eyes. I could see the evil old me looking back at me with his eyes in an expression that mimicked a violent man stepping out the prison gates with his first deep breath of freedom. Then, at that point, a total calm cascaded throughout my body, and silence gave birth within me as I stepped aside, allowing the dark side to possess me taking full control.

Instantly my veins began to pulsate as if pinning a 1000mg testosterone suspension syringe deep into my leg. Resulting in an eye-opening rage inside masked only by a smug, sick look in the mirror.

My eyes that were filled with hate, anger, and disgust were no more.

A calm, silent, serial killer demeanour had become me. Oh, this was bad. I thought.

It had been 20 minutes since I made the call to Delta Two, and it seemed the culprit had been laying low, under the bridge by the canal, where the cameras could not see him. Deciding it was safe, he started making his way across the car park when the CCTV room picked him up. "Delta Two to Charley one, we have a male fitting the description, carrying a brown leather handbag, making his way briskly across the car park."

My heart started beating ferociously as without a second thought, the dark side propelled me into a jog through the store as I calmly began to manoeuvre around people. Gradually picking up speed. My vision had become acute, weaving through customers like an expert hunter running through the woods. I started to run faster! Within seconds I was into a full sprint. Running past the royal Daulton section trying not to trash the expensive displays. Up to five stairs in one leap and towards the back door. I didn't feel in control at all, this darkness had swallowed my spirit, and all I wanted was blood. Almost not stopping, with rage enough to power my whole body straight through the hardened glass doors without opening, I entered the street. Flying past people like my life depended on it; within seconds, I was into full speed, heart rate screaming, punching the inside of my chest.

After two minutes, I had navigated across the busy primary road traffic, trying not to get run over, sliding across moving car bonnets, and jumping a small fence, landing into the car park. Sending a message to Delta Two for the suspect's location.

"Charley one from Delta Two he's just going into green town estate by the pub." I was sixty seconds from there at my current pace, and just then, I could see him turn and look back at me. "Shit, he spotted me," and now he is running. "Charley One, I'm going to lose you on camera now, I've called Zulu Mike, and they are on route."

"Delta Two, I'm going after him," panting like a crazed athlete entering the estate, my heart was beating so fast, but I felt so enraged I could tear his arms off.

I followed hot on his tail, observing him turning left down a side street. "Delta Two, he's gone, left, left into church street." "Delta Two to Charley One got that!" I just caught sight of him darting down an alleyway into the back garden of a house. Instantly turning and arriving with him, he was trying to climb the back fence to get away. Grabbing him and throwing him four foot into the air, and falling onto the grass, his stolen bag thrown across the garden.

Taking a handful of his hair and yanking his head back I screamed "Don't f****g move." Diving on him and going straight for his arm, twisting it behind his back and securing a thumb lock. He squealed like a pig as I forcefully manoeuvred him onto his knees and up into a bent-over stance with my other hand pressing on his head, ready to frog march him out into the street. He could tell by the arm lock that I was not going to be overpowered. He shouted, "Your F***g crazy you are" as I told him to "shut the f**k up!"

We stepped out onto the pavement, and I could see a patrol car at the top of the street, and seeing us, it pulled up, with two officers getting out, taking control of him and reading him his rights. I handed the bag to the officer which fit the description of the lady's handbag. Taking him into custody, the police said well done and instructed that they would later come to my store to make a statement which I was happily in agreement with.

The police car drove off, and I started to walk back to my store, having a well-deserved cigarette. After entering inside, one of the girls from cosmetics who was pretty, but looked oddly orange, asked me what had happened. I briefly explained in summary, that I had just caught the mugger of the old lady from outside, before exhaustively walking back to my office.

Once my dinner break was over, and I started my rounds again, it seemed I was now some kind of a hero to everyone who worked at the store, which came as a massive surprise to me because I didn't even think of it in that way. I was just determined to nail the scumbag, but now, it seemed I was no longer the coward they had assumed I was. Young girls that worked at the store were coming over to me and kissing me on the cheek, saying they were glad I was here to protect them, which bought tears to my eyes, to be honest.

This jungle news exclusive seemed to trickle through the town security staff as well, as individual stores contacted me to congratulate me on the arrest.

That reaction was a complete surprise to me, but it also told me how genuinely frightened the staff were of these criminals and that somehow now, they could relax with my presence. Still, one thing was evident to me, I loved catching him, it felt great, the adrenaline was the best drug feeling ever, like in the army when I was firing the SA80 on automatic, down the range. What a rush! However, little did I know then, this incident would turn out child's play compared to the coming months and years.

That night, when I got home, the first thing I asked my wife for was a grade one all over haircut. After showering, I was straight down the gym to enroll in a heavyweight training regime. The gym was full of bodybuilders, and I looked like Mr bean compared to them. Some guys were massive, leg pressing the weight of a mini car. I felt really intimidated but put them out of my mind and smashed into my two hours work out. It felt good to be training again, and all I could visualise was the criminal that had attacked me, and that powered my aggression into a great workout.

Leaving the gym, I went back into my village and called into my local for a pint. As I walked in, a group of lads who liked to think that they ran the place was throwing over evil looks and making snide remarks. You just can't get away from people like this in life; they're bloody everywhere! The best option, I thought, was just to ignore them and they will start on someone else. Still, the old me inside who now was stretching into life, ready to cause a catastrophe, was saying, they would stop if you followed them into the toilet and smashed there head off the f****g urinal until its smashed into pieces on the floor! Then how f*****g hard would they be?

Trying to ignore this impulse and remember, I promised my mom that I would only go to prison for someone worth it, and none of these wannabe Rocky Balboas was.

My good friend, Nigel, came into the bar, he was in his late fifties, an ex-hells angel, I think he said he was. A great fisherman, a right laugh, and always a friendly face, we had many sessions together, and I was so pleased to see him. He was five foot eight inches, slim to medium build, bald head, tattoos on his arms with glasses. He was the type of guy who was a loyal friend and would always have your back. We got talking about my day, and I told him a little about what had happened, he kind of looked at me as if I was a bit crazy and didn't really say much to my surprise. I don't think he liked the police that much. We chatted about other stuff for a short while, and I bid him farewell to return home, expecting one of these lads to follow, but they chose not to.

The next day, I returned to work, looking smart with my new haircut and polished boots, with my webbing belt, pouches, and radio earpiece. Now I was listening acutely to the radio for anything I could respond too. However, secretly, I looked for the description of one male, my nemesis, and my real-life antagonist.

I couldn't wait to get my f*****g hands on him. My only genuine worry was that I would batter the shit out of him, rather than detaining him. One thing was categorically exact with no hesitation in my mind, he was f***d! Shortly after lunch that day, I heard the call: "Can Mrs Robinson come to department five please." That was a theft in progress in the lady's clothes section. Sending "Charley One to Delta Two," can you put the camera on the high street door, please?"

"Delta Two to Charley One, Yes, Yes, on now over."

As I approached, several ladies were shopping as Jane, the supervisor of that department, came to me: "She's in the changing room, took 5 items in and looks really suspicious." "She has several bags with her." "Okay, Jane, I will stand back and observe."

Ten minutes passed, and then a tall, pretty girl came out, with long brown hair, a short cream dress, well-kept blonde hair and a black leather jacket on; she walked over to the counter and put the cloths back, saying sorry, they didn't fit and exited through the glass double doors into the high street. "Charley One to Delta Two, have you got eyes on her, she's turned left, left towards the roundabout." "Delta Two to Charley One, Yes, Yes, we know her, she is Whiskey Tango." "Charley One to Delta Two, can you keep an eye on her and see if she takes anything out of her bag?" "Yes, Yes, will do Charley One."

My problem was, I had not seen clear selection, concealment, then exit with non-payment, so at this stage, there was little I could do apart from check the changing room. Upon walking into the changing room, I observed a broken electronic tag; picking it up, I asked Jane if the changing rooms are checked after everyone comes out. She said they were, by the changing room attendant.

This meant that there was enough evidence to suspect but not detain, so my plan was to follow her carefully, and if she did a runner once spotting me, I knew she had something to hide. Liaising with Delta Two, I caught up with her quickly as she turned and spotted me. Stopping and reaching into her bag, she pulled out a blue top and said: "For f*** sake, here take it."

This was a clear admission that she had stolen this item, and as such, I said "sorry, you are being detained for theft." "But I will only ban you from the store once I have filled out the paperwork." Whiskey Tango agreed to walk peacefully back to my security office within the department store, which I was happy about, as I didn't want to physically detain her. She had admitted she had stolen the item, returned it to me, and was causing me no problems; thus, I felt no need to publicly embarrass her in front of everyone.

I sent to Delta Two, "female detained, but I will only ban her from Charley One's location as I have the item and it is undamaged," "Delta Two to Charley One, Yes, Yes, understood."

Returning into my office, I asked her: "Do you have any dangerous weapons, knives, needles, or sharp items, that you wish to make me aware?" Whiskey Tango said "no." I continued, "do not put your hands in your pockets at any time, as if you do, I will see it as an act of aggression, and I will restrain you." "Do you understand?" Whiskey Tango said, "yes, I know the drill." "Please take a seat while I fill out the forms." Starting a conversation with me, Whiskey Tango said, "please don't ban me from the store; I love shopping here; it's my favourite place to Christmas shop." "I'm sorry, I said, its company policy, and you're lucky I'm not calling the police." "It's only because you have cooperated that I have decided just to ban you," as I continued to fill out the forms.

"Surely there must be something we can do about it. A type of deal? she said. As I looked in Whiskey Tangos direction, she had lifted her dress to reveal her thighs, which exposed her open legs and lacy black underwear. "My God, I thought!" "No, miss, please correct yourself appropriately." She smiled, pulling down her dress and closing her legs. "I can tell you want me," she said, "you've gone all red." "It won't be happening miss, please let's just fill in this form, and you can leave." My hands were shaking a little, becoming sweaty, and my heart was silently pounding. But I would be truthful if I didn't admit that the thought entered my mind just for half a second but was quickly dismissed as a terrible idea.

"I will give you a… (Censored)." she said, sitting upright in the chair with her mouth slightly open licking her bottom lip. Shocked and trying to hold back a smile, I cleared my throat and said, "That won't be happening either," then I proceeded to fill out the form as quickly as possible, with her details and instructing her about the ban.

She cooperated, took the paperwork off me, smiled, gave me a look, pausing to connect directly into my eyes, and said "Shame," as she brushed close to me slowly as she exited my office and proceeded through the store to leave.

Turning her head back, flicking her hair, she smiled then disappeared into the busy street of shoppers. Few! Blimey! I thought as I loosened off my top button on my shirt, feeling my face rush with blood and my skin a little clammy. Never again will I go into a room alone with a female I have detained, without taking a female worker as a witness for myself and the detainee. I could have been accused of anything! She was calm, almost delightful, but proved to be dangerous in a black widow seductress way. I needed a cigarette after that encounter.

Later that day, I was in the cafeteria when I had an urgent call for assistance from Bravo One on my store watch radio. Leaving my food, I quickly manoeuvred down the stairs, and exited into the high street, accelerating into a fast run towards the door of Bravo One.

As I entered Bravo One's location, I looked around the shop floor for the girl with the store watch radio, when I heard a scream and a crash! As I focused on the area it had come from, I could see a 6ft lad running towards the doors where I was standing, then in clear eyesight, behind him, I observed a girl with a radio injured with blood on her face, screaming, STOP HIM!

I had one or two seconds to react, leaning my body as if I was falling sideways, his force forward contacted my body, where I was able to flick him completely over as my body acted like a foot tripping him. He landed on his back, as designed, but still holding him, now looking down at him, I was able to control his head from whiplashing the floor, which is a downside of this maneuverer if I wasn't careful.

This knocked the wind out of him, and he appeared somewhat subdued, as I turned him over by a reverse arm-twist, locking his arm behind his back. Now face down and airways clear, he was safely detained. Bringing him first to his knees, then on a count of three up on to his feet. I escorted him to the back of Bravo One's store into the holding room as we waited for the police to arrive.

Bravo One's security girl Sarah had been head-butted, she was in shock and emotional but was trying to calm down and be brave. The paramedics arrived shortly after the police. More statements were taken, and gratitude is given. I left Bravo One to return to my store, happy that I had been able to help, but I was disappointed that I appeared too late.

As I arrived back, walking through the Royal Doulton section, I was stopped by Karen, who told me that several paperweights had been stolen, although she couldn't say precisely when? The rest of that afternoon was watching over hours of videotapes for Karen's section, looking for suspicious behaviour, but three hours later, nothing was found on film. It was now time for the store to close, but another scumbag detained.

That night, I was in the mood for a good drink and found myself in my local where the larger was going down like milk. It was a cute little pub with a canal running past it where you could view it from the bench window. Narrowboats would pass, and people would wave jealousy as you slurped on your beer next to the always burning log fire. The landlady was funny, and her husband was a real nice guy and a great cook too. I propped myself at the bar on a stool and reflected on the day I had when this guy walked in. He was very smart looking, very handsome for a guy with a Gordon Ramsey look; he could have been his double. He was very polite, charismatic, and said hello to everyone.

What a nice guy, I thought! As I started a conversation with him, he offered me a pint, and I said, "oh no, it's okay," when he said, "no, I will get you one in for later." "What's your name?" "Hugh, he said, nice to meet you," as he put out his hand to shake mine. "Malcolm, nice to meet you too." "Do you live around here I asked?" "Sure! I live just around the corner." We sat for a while and exchanged in pleasantries, to which I found out he was a top director of sales. We clicked so well, it was like finding your best mate that you had lost for years, everything about him, I admired. I secretly wished I could be him, I guess, but I was happy to be his new friend, and I expressed my sadness when he had to leave, when he said he could often be found here propping up the bar.

As he was leaving, I followed him outside to have a cigarette, and he walked over to a Porsche 911 turbo convertible. My jaw dropped, what a beautiful car, something I could only ever dream about, I thought. He reversed out with his vehicle playing the note of pure envy, and it purred off into the estate. What a very cool guy he was, I thought, I really like Hugh! I hope I see him again soon.

Over the weekend, I had planned to compete in a regular fishing competition that I was very fond of, with my mate Nigel. He was the bailiff at the lake, and over several years, he had taught me everything I needed to know about feeder rod fishing for carp. I enjoyed nothing more than the excitement of competition carp fishing for money over a three- or five-hour match. It was my very own happy place, tranquility, coffee, sandwiches, pork pies, and plenty of cigarettes. I had made a lot of friends at the regular matches. Still, when you start to win a lot, you get to see everyone give off a big "For F***k sake, every time you pull up at 06.30 in the morning, then fewer and fewer people start to talk to you, but it's always a pleasing feeling when you're handed over their money at the end once you win.

 Nigel used to like it when I won because it meant a big piss up at the pub later that evening, and we always shared our drinking tabs. Sometimes I would buy him loads, and occasionally he would do the same for me.

Homelife was getting tenser, and I was feeling more alone in my own mind. Sometimes people grow apart, but I knew that it was having a more severe effect on my wellbeing than I was willing to admit, and I am sure my wife felt the same. Obviously, I loved my children, but I could feel a real distance growing between us all. Avoidance was a place called the gym, pub, and work, it reduced the arguing, and at the same time, I'm sure inflamed it.

I was getting fitter and stronger as the weeks of running and heavyweight sessions past. Always thinking of my real-life antagonist to which I had played out our reunion a hundred times in my head, what I would do when I get my hands on him. By now, I was running 5 miles every day with a two-hour workout four days a week. Watching these bodybuilders in the gym was like being in the company of Hollywood stars; they were massive! One night when I was at home, I investigated anabolic steroids on the internet, and to my surprise, you could order them from lots of sites and at an excellent price. What if I had their strength? Their massive arms and sturdy legs? No one would dare try to take me down then. My mind was made up; I ordered Anabol 50mg and Dianabol 10 mg each tablet. Now, this was a brilliant oral combination, and it would give me six weeks supply. Feeling excited and incredibly pleased with myself, I waited for the parcels to arrive. I imagined myself looking like a rock of toned muscle, and having blistering speed, which would be perfect for my encounters with crack fueled criminals.

I had a best friend called Jim, whom I met while working as head chef when he knocked on my kitchen door and said: "Hi Chef, you got a job?" "I can work in kitchens." He was about 5ft 5 inches, white male, brown hair, with glasses and a very playful cheeky nature. We needed someone, so as I thought he was a nice guy and I could work with him. I said "yes." The next day he started work and proved to be a good lad and hardworking, his culinary knowledge was limited, but he made up for that with his wacky sense of humour. On finishing his first day, he asked if he could put on a cd to clean up. Ultra-Violence Hardcore Mother Fucker. Well, I laughed, "what the hell is that" I said? Jim just laughed. That night he invited me to a house party at his. Not needing any excuse for the avoidance of going home, I agreed, and three hours later, I was lying flat on the pavement outside his house after turning green from trying a cannabis joint. I felt like I was dying, and Jim thought he had killed his boss on his first day.

After that, Jim and I became close friends, although Jim had many friends and was extremely popular, partly because of his rational nature and his enthusiasm for happiness and parties. It also was a surprise to hear that he was very highly skilled in Bushido, some obscure samurai style of fighting, but being the wise old man in a young body, he never really talked about it. I could always rely on a bed and some beers anytime I called round to Jim's, and occasionally a hulk throwing up session in his toilet.

A few days past and I had come home to two parcels. Great, they are here! After reading the instructions very carefully, I swallowed down the maximum dose with a pint of water, got changed for the gym, and headed eagerly for the big weights, allowing the one-hour consumption process to filter through into my bloodstream. I didn't feel anything, to begin with, but after an hour, I started to feel it rushing through my body. My arms were getting massive, and I wasn't experiencing any fatigue at all; in fact, my two-hour session went to three, and I became angrier and more intense with every weight I lifted.

Crowbar Robbery

The next morning, I woke feeling like a train had hit me, struggling to get out of bed, but after another hefty dose of steroids, I slowly started to feel re-energized, entering work ready for another day of surprises. I was continuously thinking, would this be the day that I meet Whiskey Kilo, the one who attacked me? I was still filled with fury towards him and felt scared but enraged thinking of our reunion, what I would do, and would I be able to keep to the right side of the law?

The early afternoon that day, I recall the radio breaking the silence with the most horrible call. "All call signs, Emergency Assistance in Whiskey One's location!"

I could hear in her voice she was panting for breath with her shaky words and a tone that I could tell she was in deep distress.

Whiskey one was sixty seconds from my back door of the department store. I immediately started running through the clothing section towards the back door, exiting into the street, I sent a message through my radio saying, "Charley One responding." My heart was pounding. My breath was already heavy with nervous anticipation with massive amounts of adrenaline due to the unknown fear of what I was going to run into and the combination of a high dose of breakfast steroids.

As I entered the store, I observed eight customers, one with two small children. The girl with the radio said to me that there were four men upstairs breaking into the staff lockers with crowbars, stealing the staff's personal items, and taking their pay packets, which they had received today.

Without thinking, I flew up the stairs, ready for an instant confrontation; at the top of the stairs, I met another staff member who said they were in this room, as she pointed to a closed door. I collected myself for one moment. I quietly sent through the radio "Charley One to Delta Two," four men reported at Whiskey One's location, armed with crowbars and theft in progress, Charley one on-site and going in." Approaching the door handle, I burst into the room, to observe it was empty! "Where are they? I asked the girl?" "They were here a minute ago," she said. The room was open, with a door that was locked going into another room. "Where does this door go," I asked?

"Into another store," she said, "but it's always locked." As I left the room, I heard someone banging about through another door. "What's in here, I asked?" "The toilet," she said, "I think one is hiding in there trying to get out of the window."

Instantly banging on the door, I shouted, "I'm requesting you step out of this toilet, slowly showing me your hands." Silence came from the bathroom. Again, I banged on the door, this time with great force. "Step out of the toilet now, or I will force open the door." I could hear movement, but no voices answered me. Bang, bang, bang, I slammed my hand on the door again, shouting "step back from the door now and come out, showing me your hands." There was a short pause of silence when I heard the door being unlocked. I stepped back, ready to be attacked with some crazed trapped criminal holding a crowbar and cornered like an angry badger.

The door slowly opened, I braised, ready to counter strike, suddenly a small boy, perhaps six years old, scared, stepped out of the toilet. My heart sank as I kneeled to his height. "Are you okay." I asked? "I'm so sorry." "Take my hand, and I will take you downstairs to your parents." This was not something I was looking forward to doing, the poor lad was obviously frightened, and I felt so sorry. I walked over to his father, holding his hand, and said, "I'm so terribly sorry, your son was in the toilet as a theft was in progress upstairs, and I was lead to believe that one of the offenders was in the toilet, so I banged on the door several times, and I'm afraid I have scared your son." He looked at his son, who was quiet and then looked at me with a face of complete disapproval, taking his son into his arms and turning away in a silent voice to say, "I think you better get out of my sight."

Upstairs, still feeling awful about the young boy, I observed there were lockers broken open, but there was no sign of offenders anywhere. The girl with the radio was still upstairs, and I asked her, "what has happened?" "Where have they gone?" "I have no idea." she said. "They have just vanished."

Returning in a slow walk back to my store and sending Delta Two the information that the offenders had fled the scene and no apparent direction or location of their whereabouts were known. I still felt awful about the boy, and I recall reflecting how acting on another person's information could have led to a more severe outcome. "What if I had kicked in the door?"

It was a clarification in a big way that I must be more careful; hurting anyone was not my intention, and this would be something I would remember, never to trust one person's assumptions. Later that day, I had a phone call from Delta Two, informing me that the offenders had a key to the inside door of that room that led to another store's department and that is how they all got away clean, through this door, locking it as they escaped.

The situation was still raw in my mind as I did my patrols around the store later that day. "What would I have done if I entered that room with four criminals with crowbars?" I could have been killed. I didn't overthink this, as my state of mind was already starting to affect my judgment. I didn't care about myself, only about protecting other people and the capture and detainment of these rats that cause so much misery, every day to innocent people. All I was focused on was my own personal war against them, and my war had only just started.

Later that night, I found myself back in my local pub; I didn't want to go to the gym this night, as I wanted my muscles to have time to heal, allowing the muscle fibres to mend and strengthen. When I entered, I observed my mate Nigel was already tucking away his third or fourth beer. He was pleased to see me, and we talked about things in general, and how my job was. I didn't want to tell him about my day today, as I was still feeling somewhat ashamed and embarrassed.

We laughed and talked about darts and fishing, while I tucked into several pints, washing away my day of days. As always in a bar, when the door swings open, everyone looks, and this time it was Hugh! He walked in, and everyone all looked at him as he stepped over to the bar with his big smile, sporting his Gordon Ramsey hairstyle, looking immaculately dressed in his pinstriped suit, his highly polished shoes, pink shirt, and maroon tie.

It was like royalty had just walked in. "Wow I said, look at Hugh" "You look, brilliant mate." holding out my hand and shaking his. Smiling at me, he said, "cheers mate, do you fancy a beer?" "No, let me buy you one," I replied, and we settled into a light-hearted conversation about what he had been up to and how his work was? Nigel, on the other hand, did not seem impressed at all as he moved away from us a few places down the bar. Did he know him, I thought?

Is there something I don't know about Hugh? Not letting this bother me, I continued to catch up with Hugh, not wanting to ignore Nigel, but he had visually already said in his body language that he didn't wish to be a part of our conversation.

I have always believed that you should treat everyone as you find them. If people have done no wrong to you, you should treat them as you would like to be treated, so I happily continued talking to Hugh, and minute by minute, I was bonding strongly with his views and his charismatic demeanour. It was apparent that I greatly admired his presence, and I desperately wanted to be his friend. We talked and drank for an hour or so, not really saying anything to Nigel, who had turned his back to us and was in a conversation with someone else.

Then Hugh said he must go, but said I will see you soon, "are you in on Saturday?" "I will come up at around 6pm." "Yes, I said, I will meet you here, and we can have a bit of a session." Smiling at me, he shook my hand and said how nice it was to see me again, and we can catch up on Saturday. As before, I followed him out to have a cigarette, and once again, dribbled over his Porsche convertible. Hugh lite up a cigarette too and said, "would you like to come around to my house one day and meet his wife and kids?" "Yes, I said instantly, I would love that." We talked some more while we finished our cigarettes, he bid me farewell and jumped into his Rolex watch of a car.

"Wow, I thought, I can't wait to have a ride in that," as he carefully purred out of the car park. I went back into the bar to find Nigel, who was rather frosty as he spoke to me and made a comment that Hugh was "terrible news." "Why" I asked? "Just trust me, he's bad news." "You need to stay away from him." he said.

I was taken aback by this comment, and thought, what is Nigel's problem? Hugh is a lovely guy! Nigel must be jealous? The atmosphere had changed by then, and I finished off my pint and decided to go home, saying bye to everyone and Nigel before the short walk back. What was Nigel's problem? I thought, Strange!

Work had been quiet for a few days, not much happening apart from further incidents in the town, far from my store, which I had heard over the store watch radio. I had heard Whiskey Kilos name mentioned a couple of times, and that had put me on high alert, although no sightings close to me. Several others were active, but it seemed word was getting out to avoid my store. The more proactive I was being observed, the less they appeared to want to take a chance with me, which was reassuring. Although I wished to have the chase, the adrenaline, the cat, and mouse game, I would have to wait for the moment.

I was becoming very fond of two girls in the store, charming I might add, gorgeous in fact, but I was cautious not to be seen talking too much with them as this would be frowned upon. My relationship was still strained with my wife, and I missed the sweet feeling of being close to someone. At no point, of course, would I ever suggest that my wife was somewhat to blame. She was always a great mother and did her best in her own way; it was just something that was happening to us gradually as time passed. It was probably mostly my fault, and I would do anything to avoid arguments, meaning I was always out.

I remember feeling sad inside, unloved with no intimacy, and this set a cold, rejected feeling within me, which often meant I was inconsiderate. I would often see my mate Jim, and end up, after too many beers, sleeping on his floor or couch and not returning home until the next day as I wouldn't drive when I had been drinking. Often without phoning her to tell her where I was, which I am not proud of. I understand how thoughtless that was, but when boys start drinking and time passes, having a great time, it's easy to turn off your phone as you do not wish to be in an argument in front of your mates, spoiling your evening. However, I know that does not make it right. If the roles were to be reversed, I would have been frantic. Yes, I could be an asshole at times.

Friday came around quickly, I was getting excited to meeting up with Hugh again on Saturday in the local pub.

Back at work after another great workout at the gym early morning that day, I started to fill out. My arms were looking massive from all the dumbbell curls and beam pull-ups, still on the maximum load, I felt no aches or pains. I was feeling more robust by the day, although I was starting to sweat a lot, and my core temperature seemed to be continually running high as I was often red-faced, and it appeared I had a rash forming on my chest.

On Friday afternoon, I was in court giving evidence against the lad who had injured the radio girl in Bravo One, which was short and sweet, reading out of my black notebook, which I filled in after every incident. Walking back through the town, where there is often traffic congestion, I suddenly heard shouting. Looking in the direction of the event, I could not believe my eyes. There was a male, kicking a heavily pregnant woman in the stomach across three lanes of traffic on the other side of the road. At first, I couldn't believe what I had just seen, but as his foot raised again, I started to dash across the street, then out of nowhere, this guy jumped out of a taxi and pinned him to the floor. Good for him, I thought. Later I gave a statement to the police, and this male was locked up. What goes on in people's minds I will never understand.

Back in the store, my manager had said, we had more paperweights stolen that day. It seemed my store was being watched for when I left the building. I would have to be careful from now on.

After everyone had left, I got into my car and drove home that Friday afternoon, although not far as I quickly had to stop due to a grinding noise coming from my car. After inspection, a sinking feeling came over me. All my wheels nuts had been loosened. I was missing three of the four on each wheel. It was clear, someone wanted me severely injured or dead! But who? Which one of the criminals I had detained was it? Or was its Whiskey Kilo? After pulling over, parking, and walking to Halfords, I managed to replace the wheel nuts by taking one into the store. I was not happy, but more so, I was now anxious. Could someone really want me dead? It appeared there was a strong possibility this was the case.

Saturday was a great day of fishing with Nigel in a local competition, although I never mentioned Hugh or that he was coming to the pub that night. We had a great match, Nigel won, and I came third, which meant that our beer was taken care of. Nigel was a great fisherman and made it look effortless. Packing up, we agreed to meet at 6pm sharp as we ventured home to wash the smell of fish and ground bait off before getting into some smart clothes and heading to the pub.

I would often cook dinner, being an ex-chef, and make sure I played with my children for an hour or so. My wife and I didn't really have many conversations, although we would always try to be polite in front of the children.

Ready for a great night, I entered the pub and started my one arm pull-ups with their most excellent beer with high expectations of meeting Hugh again. That night, he didn't show up, and I was gutted. However, Nigel and I had a great night, laughing, singing, and eating hot pork pies and mushy peas at the bar. The bar was full of characters, and one lady I used to talk to was called Sadie. She was a cancer survivor and had a brilliant personality; she had permed hair and glasses about five foot four with a medium to large frame but had a unique tone to her voice. She would swear at you if she so wished and tell you to get her a drink, which I always found amusing; I liked Sadie, salt of the earth as they say, also a good pisshead.

I must admit, deep down, I was disappointed Hugh couldn't come; I had waited days to see him again, but something must have come up.

Sunday was time for another fishing match with an early start at 7am, which was never right after a night full of beer. Unfortunately, I pulled a crap peg out of the bag and had little chance to win that day, but persevered and ended up with a beautiful few and still had a good day anyway. Nigel come second, which meant only one thing, into the bar early tonight for another mild session.

On a Sunday, Quiz night was always funny but rubbish as well, as we never could win, but there is still that team in the corner every week who just pop in for the quiz and take the prize money! Twats! We were only jealous. Although that wasn't going to stop us from having another great night of laughter and tales.

It was November time now, and the cold dark nights were heating things up at work, as by 4pm CCTV were struggling to spot the criminals in their parker coats and hoodies, which was making for exciting sport. An emergency assistance call from Mike One left a sour taste in my mouth when I responded to see the guard of the store, Ian, struggling with a male outside his store. Before I could get to him, he had launched this guy in an overly aggressive way, entirely over his shoulders coming hard flat on the concrete. A great technique, I must say, but against all the rules of detainment.

We are supposed to detain, causing no injury to ourselves or the criminal, which was clearly not what I had seen. CCTV had him caught on camera too, and it was looking like he would get sacked or have a massive bollocking off the town centre police officer, if not charged with assault. Ian was a young lad about 22 years old and so bloody handsome. He looked just like the actor from fast and furious films, Paul Walker, and probably could have been a model; why he chose to work in security, I'm unaware. He was a nice lad, but this was a big mistake.

I later found out that he was verbally disciplined and managed to get off lightly as he was being attacked but was cautioned that he had used excessive force to control the situation. Ian would not respond to calls for help for some time after that after his store manager grounded him to the store itself for a cooling-off period.

Sierra One was a food superstore not far from mine; the guard in there was called Carl, a very experienced and a stocky built lad, a bit like a bull terrier but slow on his feet due to his large stature.

A call for help come through late that evening from Sierra One, and I made my way down to the store, ensuring CCTV had the cameras on the doors. Once inside, feeling slightly out of breath after the quick dash through the town and across a busy main road, I met with Carl. He had already detained an individual and was escorting him towards the back office. I assisted in walking alongside him and his detainee to enforce the presence of security. Arriving at the office, Carl called for Police attendance to come to the store as one IC1 male had been detained, which is radio speak for one white male.

The male was not known to us; he was six-foot of medium build, with a worn and tired look upon his face, a bomber jacket black in colour, and greasy dark, messy hair. I presumed he was from out of town. I could see as he sat in the holding room, the male was looking twitchy, his right knee bouncing up and down as he sat, and his eyes were looking at the exit and the window. Carl started to fill out the paperwork, and I stood in front of him, cautioning him to keep his hands out of his pockets and asking him if he had any sharps on him, which included anything that could be used as a weapon against us? He started with the verbal abuse, swearing at me, calling me all the vulgar names he could think of. I was not concerned with this; I was too busy watching his body language.

I could sense an invisible atmosphere that things were about to turn nasty, although Carl, with his back to me, seemed unaware. The male was winding himself up, the aggression building in his voice. Carl told him to calm down, but it made no difference. I knew any second now he could attack us. Then in the middle of another barrage of abuse, putting his hand into his right coat pocket, I grabbed him by his left arm, pulling off the chair and hard onto the floor of the office before Carl had time to react. His right arm was still in his pocket, but now he was face down on the floor and kicking off like crazy, his left arm bent straight in a twisted arm lock and my right foot pressing his left shoulder to the floor. He was screaming and swearing that he was going to kill me and trying to breakdance his body off the floor with considerable force.

I knew I had to secure the arrest more and bent his arm into his back with a thumb lock, to which he let out a significant scream of pain. I asked Carl to carefully check his right pocket by moving his right arm into a spiral and observing his pocket contents. It was a used needle with black stuff inside the syringe with a layer of what looked like blood lining the inner plastic tube. I later found out it was the remains of heroin combined with his blood. He remained on the floor until two officers came to arrest him shortly after, and the broken DVDs he had attempted to remove the security tag from were taken with him to the station.

I was asked to call into the station to make a statement before I went home that day, which was becoming an almost everyday thing. Although I just viewed it as contributing just a little to keeping the public safe. Reflecting on this last arrest, I was happy, but also sombre, thinking when would be the next time that happens, and would I be so lucky to spot and sense the move in time? I even thought of looking into a stab vest, as this may be a good idea.

That evening I stayed home with my wife and kids for the first time in a while, as I was conscious that my job was dangerous. Sitting and playing with my kids somewhat diffused the darkness I had growing inside of me. As they giggled and jumped around, it was nice to see pure love within them, not tainted by the world, not angry or stained, just innocence. I did enjoy those moments.

I was still taking my full dose of steroids, not eating that great, often loaded up in the evenings with alcohol and smoking maybe fifteen a day. My emotional wellbeing was at an all-time low; my hands were starting to shake, not from alcohol, but from the steroids as they taxed my immune system, draining my body of the nutrients and water to fuel and build the muscle tissue I forced to grow.

I planned a good session in the gym the following morning before work. I got bigger and more powerful, but I still felt like more Mr Bean compared to the other injecting bodybuilders in the gym. However, I tried not to look at them and just got on with my military-style workout, but I would always catch a glimpse of them and admire how fantastic they looked. They looked like the Hulk, and I dreamed of one day looking that great too. It was a little hard to imagine this coming true unless I increased my dosing and protein shake intake, so I decided to do it when I got home. I knew deep within that what I was doing was careless and dangerous, but I have always been a risk-taker.

The following day at work, Crystal, a girl from the lingerie department, was making eyes at me, well, that's what I thought. I had never been that great at reading women, then again, has any man? She was flirting with me; I was sure of it. She was about 23 years old, slim, and always smartly dressed—Smelling of strawberries with her long ginger hair. I certainly fantasized in my mind what it would be like to have a girl like her on my arm. Still, I just thought it was work style flirting that would come to nothing. Nevertheless, men can sometimes be pretty stupid when it comes to what women want and desire, or should I correct myself and say in my own personal experience with women, meaning I have been stupid at reading signals.

I wondered about Hugh and if he was okay? I was still keen to be welcomed into his world, and I looked forward to meeting his family if that chance manifested. I hoped I would see him later in the local.

The rest of the day was uneventful, attending to assist one incident in the market where the lady security guard had some lip from some unruly teenagers. The guards in the shopping centre were not from our elite unite and were, let's say, somewhat lethargic when it comes to being proactive towards offenders, and they didn't like me chasing people through their territory.

That afternoon, it was dark when I was walking to my car, I felt uneasy about something. The wind was bitter, stinging my face as it whipped over the open park, where I had parked my car. Approaching my car, I could see the shapes of people standing around it. At first, I thought nothing of it, until getting closer, I recognized they were from the local homeless shelter—five of them in total, all holding what appeared to be sticks and planks of wood.

I did think of turning and running, but if I showed any fear, I would give them power over me. One male approached me as I stood and shouted as loud as I could in a drill, sergeant manner. "Stop! Stand back! Holding my hand outstretched in a clear sign for him to understand. He began to give me a barrage of abuse as the others stood behind him. He was telling me that my cards were marked and if I detained any more of them, I would be put into the hospital.

I could sense their apprehension, so I catapulted forward at this male, spinning my back around, so I was facing away from him, grabbing the plank of wood with my right hand and elbowing his chest in a reverse thrust pushing him on to my car bonnet. Now I had the plank of wood, the others started to run, as I screamed at them in the craziest psychotic growl I could muster. The lad on the bonnet was called Tango Bravo, and he limped off in a winded retreat. I thought about chasing them, but that would have been wrong as they were no longer a danger to me as they were running away from me.

Throwing the wooden plank to the gutter, I got into my car and drove home. This kind of thing was expected, the more of a reputation I was getting, the higher chance of attacks, but that was a price I was prepared to pay if it meant continuing my war against them. However, always now, I was on my guard, waiting, wondering when my luck would run out, which was an unsettling feeling and a very lonely one. F**k them, I thought, they started this, when they attacked me if I'm scaring and upsetting them all, excellent!

Back into the gym later that evening for a marathon of a session. After consuming my supplements, I was raging, smashing the weights to the loud sound of club music vibrating around the gym.

By now, people were starting to notice I was on something as my workouts were getting more massive and intense. All I could focus on was that future meeting with the scumbag who attacked me.

I was feeling strong, overgrowing, pumped, and aggressive, ready for a fight with anybody. Three hours later and feeling jacked, I would just stop for a quick pint on the way home.

Walking into the pub, the group of lads were there instantly giving me the evil looks. In a spontaneous rage, I snapped! "You lot can F***k off!" I shouted at them. "The day I've had today, I will throw you through the F****g window!"......Silence fell over the whole pub as I turned my back to them and apologized to the bar lady. "I'm sorry, but I've had enough shit today love, I don't need it as soon as I walk into my local." "Just calm down, Malc," she said. Have a beer and chill out. I could hear them chuntering behind me, and I would occasionally turn giving them evil looks, but to be honest, I was sick of people like that who prey on people they think are weaker than them. They're nothing short of bullies, and my steroid fueled temperament was not up for any of their bullshit tonight.

I welcomed them to follow me outside as I left; perhaps this was the quickest way of sorting this shit out? But they decided against it, I think they were thinking I was unbalanced asking them all outside, but as is always in life, stand up to the bullies and they back down because they are cowards, just like the scum running around the towns and cities hurting vulnerable people. I hate them all!

After I had calmed down at home, which took me abnormally about two hours, I reflected on what I had said with my outburst in the pub. That's not who I usually am; I'm usually a very calm and laid-back guy. One of two things was happening: The steroid use was affecting my aggression, or the constant fact that everyone seemed to want to hurt me everywhere was starting to change me or perhaps both. I was changing, though; I could feel myself agitated, on the defence and sad inside. Surely that would be a normal response to someone experiencing gangs of lads surrounding their car and individuals trying to beat them up or sabotaging your car wheels or trying to stick you with a needle? Unlike police officers, I didn't have counselling, pepper spray, batons, cuffs, or even backup, but that's how it was. I could always stay in my store and not respond to help? But how can an ex-soldier ever do that? I could quit and go do something else? No, it was too late now, I was in it till the end, no matter what, and I had a score to settle.

Two days later, at work, I would be thrown into my biggest challenge, yet when I would find myself in an all-out brawl against three criminals in the centre of my town. Foxtrot One had a triple bulk snatch and screamed down the store watch radio for urgent assistance as they made off into the town centre. After hearing the descriptions and the direction in which they were travelling. I accelerated into a sprint down the opposite road at my store's side to intercept them. As they entered the town centre, I could see them in plain view, walking quickly with their jackets bulging tucked into their trousers to hide the stolen stock.

Within seconds I was in between them all, grabbing two of them by their coats and bringing them to a halt. Furious, they started to pull away, and at that point, the stolen items of frozen food, which were joints of meat, fell out of their jackets onto the floor.

I had already called CCTV to monitor my movements, and I knew I was being observed. One lad took a swing at me, narrowly missing my face as my response was a clean leg sweep putting him on his arse. The second lad came in for a head butt connecting unfortunately with my elbow as I spun to the left with my arm diagonal in front of his neck, sending him backwards on top of the guy on the floor. The third guy landed a kick to my side, which in return, I followed with a leg sweep on the other leg, which he had all his balance on, dropping him to the floor. The lads on the floor were trying to get up when I dragged the third lad on top of them. By now, there was frozen meat everywhere, and guards hearing what was going on over the store watch radio were starting to assist me. There were many threats to kill me and that my family was dead and all that usual bullshit. But in the end, three were detained for theft by officers in a nearby patrol car.

Nursing a painful side, I hobbled back to my store, feeling good that I was starting to really piss these criminals off and play a part in getting these individuals off the street, but I could not help think, deep down, that they won't be letting this go. My darker side would give a response in my head clear and robust: "F*** Them!

After a coffee and a cigarette, I continued my patrols, and later an officer came to collect a statement from me. This took some time, and then the day was gone. It was time to get off home.

Within an hour, I was out running again around my village, which was a good run achieving four miles without stopping. I was clearly getting fitter and more robust, but I thought I would leave the gym tonight as my cardio was enough.

Arriving in the pub at about 7pm, I was elated to see Hugh at the bar. Oh, I was so pleased, and we got straight into a great conversation while I polished off three pints rather quickly. I asked Hugh if he knew Nigel, and he said he did. He knew many people in the village. I asked him why he thought Nigel didn't like him? Hugh said: "I was cornered by three of the lads who thought they owned the village one night in the car park of this pub." "What they didn't realize was that I was a light heavyweight boxer," as he laughed. "Two of them went down very quickly, and the third ran off." "One of these lads was a relation to Nigel, and since then, many people in the village don't like me."

I thought his story was brilliant and said, "good for you." He laughed some more, and we continued to drink some of the night away, getting closer and closer as our opinions and principles seemed to match. Hugh then said he had to leave and go back to his family but asked if I would like to come around to his house? I said, "I would love to." "Friday night at 7pm, it is then." he said, and after telling me his address, we shook hands again and said our goodbyes. I felt a powerful connection to Hugh. He was smart, kind, intelligent, and successful, something that I also strived to be in life, but he had made it. I run after criminals for a living, and he uses his brain to earn five times a month what I receive in my salary.

I admired him greatly, and he could look after himself, which was an added quality. Finishing a few more beers and deciding to take a Chinese home, I made my way back via the takeaway and surprised my wife with a token of kindness. I settled down that evening, internally thinking to myself how much I was looking forward to Friday. I wondered if we would go out. What would we do? If we would go out in his Porsche? What should I wear even entered my mind? I hope his wife likes me.

Dancing with the Devil

The following day at work was quiet, as the nights were here to stay, it was almost December now, and the Christmas shopping was in full swing. As I was standing at my back door, observing who was hanging around, I noticed an elderly gentleman walking on his own, who started to crouch over and fall on the pavement. Sending the information to Delta Two to get the cameras on me, I approached the gentleman lying on his side. Carefully turning him on his back, I observed that he appeared to be not breathing! Checking his pulse in his wrist and his neck, my horror was confirmed. Sending to Delta Two, I needed a paramedic; I started CPR on him, practicing ten compressions to five breaths, which I had been taught many years ago in the Army. However, when I got to the breath part, an observer said she was a nurse and that I should not do the breath part and concentrate on compressions only. Taking her advice, I started CPR, and after two minutes, the gentleman began to breathe again, and his eyes opened. I reassured him everything would be okay and turned him into the recovery position, which I thought would be the best course of action, although he stopped breathing again within a minute of doing this.

Returning him onto his back, I began CPR again, while hearing a call on my store watch radio that the paramedics were on route. Still, ten compressions with a gap of five seconds to check for any breath, I continued to do this for three minutes, and to my relief, he started breathing again, and once more, his eyes opened. Hearing the sirens echoing off the buildings as the paramedics drew closer, I tried to make him comfortable. I continued to talk to him, but sadly he stopped breathing again just as the paramedics pulled up. Continuing CPR and briefing the paramedic on what was happening, he got out a defibrillator.

He commenced working on him with this machine, but to no avail, finally deciding to get him into his paramedic vehicle and leaving, sirens blazing for the hospital.

My hands were shaking after that incident; I needed a coffee and a cigarette.

Three hours later, I managed to call the hospital to ask about the gentleman; however, the nurse on the phone did not want to give me any information as I was not a family member. After explaining what had happened, she put me on hold and a couple of minutes later come back to say: The gentleman in question has stabilized and is sitting up in bed talking to his wife.

This was fantastic news, and I was so happy to hear this. The last thing anyone would want is to die alone on a cold, dark winter night in a town centre side street. At least he got to speak with his wife and hold her hand. I don't know how his future worked out after that day, but I hope it turned out well.

A few days later, the paramedic man came to see me and said that he was recommending me for an ambulance commendation, which he said involved publicity and my picture in a paper. I kindly declined as there were too many people looking to harm me because of the nature of my job, and more public attention could put me at risk. He understood.

A few days later, I received a letter from the board of directors for the store I worked in, a certificate from my security boss, and a kind letter from the Mayor, which was nice.

I remember staying home that night, cuddling my kids, and being a dad for once. Sometimes, I would get lost inside and forget what's important in life.

Friday came around fast, and it would be tonight. I would meet Hugh's family, which I was really looking forward to. It was a dark, gloomy day at work, with the wind rattling the doors and people running in windswept from the streets. Bravo One called my call sign and asked if I could make my way to the store, which I did, but it appeared not urgent by the nature of the request, so a briskly walked. Attending and meeting Peter, who had a store radio, he said that he had detained a girl and wanted assistance if I didn't mind? "Sure, where is she?" "In the holding room." As I entered, I observed this young girl about eleven years old, sitting somewhat scared looking. "Oh, I said, what have you been up to?" "I stole some fake eyelashes." "What! Is that it?" "How much were they?" "Seventy-five-pence" she responded.

"Wait one moment, please." I called Peter to come back in on my store watch radio, moments later, he entered the room. "Peter, why are you detaining this girl for theft of fake eyelashes?" "why don't you just ban her from the store?" "It's company policy now that everyone who commits a theft must be handed over to the police." "Are you crazy, Peter?" "Do you know what this will do to her and her life because she has made a stupid mistake?" "She's a child for god sake." Also, where is her female independent person?" "Why is she not present?" "I will just go and get her." he said.

I knew the fire escape was next to the holding room, and I watched Peter walk right down to the bottom of the store. "What's your

name?" I asked her. "Kate" she answered. "Right, Kate" I never
want to see you in this store again, do you understand?" "err yes, she
responded. "Right, come with me." She got up, and we turned left
out of the detaining room to the fire exit door, which led to the car
park and the ally way. "Go," I said, "now run and don't stop till your
away from here." She flew out the door like a whippet out a trap, and
I was pleased she had got away. Although I knew Peter would not
be. I told Peter that I went to the toilet and when I came back, she
was gone; I don't think he believed me, but he got onto his radio and
cancelled the police attending. Later that day, Peter sent a message
"Bravo One to Charley One." "Charley One receiving, go ahead,
Peter." "Just wanted to thank you for earlier. Our fire exit door had
been sticking; I see on our video that you were able to fix it for us."

Silence responded for what seemed a minute until I returned,
"Charley One to Bravo One, always happy to help, received over."
Peter obviously was not pleased.

After lunch and doing my rounds up and down my store, I was called
by Mike One: "Charley One from Mike One, are you receiving
over?" "Yes, Mike One, go ahead, please." "Charley One, can you
attend my store." "I have theft in progress." "On route Mike One."
as I picked up speed through the ladies' clothing section, watched by
all the customers as I flew out of the front doors and down the street,
entering Mike One's location within a minute. Sending "Charley one
in your area now Mike One, where are you?" "Food section Charley

One," he replied. As I approached, Mike One met up with me and said an IC1 female acted suspiciously in the food area. She was 5ft 10 of very stocky build and long dark hair wearing jeans and a brown woollen jumper. He said he would go upstairs and get the internal cameras on her if I would observe from the shop floor, which I agreed. Slowly moving in to watch this lady, I could see she was aggressive, barging past old ladies and appeared to be either drunk or under the influence of drugs. Coming around one of the refrigerated units, she barged into another elderly man knocking him into a rack of clothes on the end of the aisle which joined the fridge section. That's it, I thought as I sent a message to Delta Two to put the cameras onto the front door, as I was about to escort an aggressive IC1 female out of the store. Delta Two responded and confirmed the cameras were ready.

Mike One responded to say that he had this lady on camera and to approach with caution. Stepping towards her, I told her that her behaviour was a dangerous influence on members of the public, and I asked her to calmly leave the store. Her response was a barrage of abuse at the top of her voice. Swearing and saying the most inappropriate words, I had no option but to physically grab hold of her arm by the elbow and my other hand on her wrist to lead her towards the front of the store. This gave me an instant move to reverse twist her arm behind her back if she did not cooperate. At that point, all hell broke loose as she went into a full-blown physical attack on me.

Punching me with her other fist, several times in the face, as I attempted to reverse her arm. She seemed so powerful it caught me by surprise; by this time, the fridge section was starting to be destroyed as we battled together while she was in a full-blown attack on me. Eight or nine punches had landed across my head as I increasingly thought, I'm in trouble here, this is serious, I needed to stop her. We both ended up being thrown sideways by the event into the lingerie section, flattening four rails of underwear, kicking, and punching me, she continued to come at me in a crazed psychotic way.

Now more displays had been trashed, and I knew I only had one chance to get this under control when I stepped in to do a leg sweep of both her legs, which sent her flat on her backside. She ended up in a sitting position on a wrecked shop floor, with her wrist in my left hand. The same arm elbow in my right, I pressed down on her left shoulder with my right foot, twisting her body to end with her face flat on the floor and her body face down in hundreds of pounds of knickers and bras, finally enabling a reverse arm-twist into a lock behind her back.

Joined by Mike One, we secured her more as we got her up to her feet, side kicking us and spitting in our faces; she was dragged to the door to go upstairs to the holding room, so we could secure her and move her out of public view, due to her continuing verbal abuse of us. Going up the stairs was precarious as she would kick and spit, pulling us down the stairs. In the holding room, we attempted to calm her down, but nothing would work. Still trying to kick us and spit at us, I instructed Mike One to help me detain her on the floor, where it would be safe for us. After another resisting attempt, she ended up dropping on the floor harder than we had wished due to her continually trying to assault us and throwing us off balance. In contrast, we attempted to prevent the situation from getting worse. Finally, she was still flat on the floor, airways clear, and arms locks sealed with only enough pressure to maintain her position. Trying to get out of it only resulted in more trouble, which caused her pain, and thus after a few moments, she started to calm a bit.

Police had been called through store watch. Now the manager and supervisor had turned up to the holding room, opening the door.

Oh my god, the manager said: "F*** Off" shouted the girl on the floor like a scene from the exorcist, and both shut the door sharply. She remained on the floor for approximately ten minutes until three officers turned up and attempted to take over. As I released my grip, she got up and started to attack the policemen, to which they swiftly responded and had her in cuffs. She then started to kick the police officers. To prevent this, they ended up carrying her out of the holding room. Two officers holding her legs and feet and the other officer linking his hands around her cuffed arms in a stretcher formation waddled towards the goods lift that led into the car park where their patrol cars were. Getting into the elevator with her and the three officers, we descended to the ground floor with a constant barrage of abuse from the still crazed women. They successfully placed her into the back of their police car, slamming the door, saying thank God for that!

I said I would be in shortly to make a statement and the three officers left with one arrested, cuffed crazy women.

I was physically drained, and I had sustained many injuries and bruises, but the worst was a sharp pain in my shoulder, where I believe I must have torn a ligament or a muscle when I went down with her on the shop floor. This was not good as an injury could put me in danger on my next arrest. Mike One and I shook hands, and I left him and the store girls continuing to put the store back together. The lingerie section had been flattened, perhaps six racks were now flat on the floor and knickers and bras everywhere.

Back to my store, now 4pm, I headed to the ramp for a coffee and a cigarette, feeling in pain and totally exhausted; my face was really sore where she had landed several direct punches, and my thigh was bruised where she had side kicked me maybe five or six times. I had taken a beating off this detainee, and the craziest thing about it all was she was a girl. I would later find out; she was on crack cocaine and was from a gipsy family off a caravan site at the back of the industrial estate near the town. I instantly was worried on hearing this news, as usual form would be males of the site taking revenge on the people who detained them. However, that was getting a familiar scenario for me anyway, so nothing new there.

Arriving back home that night, I felt in a lot of pain, my shoulder was killing me, and I was concerned if I would have to phone up sick the next day. Taking some painkillers and my usual steroid dose, I decided to have a long soak in the bath before going out to meet Hugh at his house.

Knocking on his door at my allocated arrival time, a pretty blonde lady answered and asked me to come in. Hugh was playing with his daughter in the front room and welcomed me to sit on the couch while his wife kindly made me a coffee. I talked with his wife, a lovely lady, and we watched his daughter play happily with her toys; she must have been about four years old.

After twenty minutes, Hugh told his wife that we were going out and that he would not be back late. She asked him where we were going, and he said to the pub for a quick one and then to see his friend. After kissing his daughter and his wife, we stepped out onto the drive where his Porsche was parked and, getting out his keys, said, "Come on, get in." Getting into his car, I was totally overcome with envy; what a beautiful car, I told Hugh. "Yes, it's beautiful, he said, but I'm thinking of changing it for an Aston Martin next month." "Really, Hugh," wow, it's so lovely!

We drove the short distance to the pub car park, parking the car, entering the warm glow of a log fire burning inside the bar.

Nigel was at the bar, and the evil looks we got were terrible. "Hi Nigel, I said," "You alright," he said? Turning his back on us. JESUS, I thought, don't need this as soon as we walk in.

Nigel went to sit down at the bottom of the pub, and Hugh and I stood at the bar and ordered a drink. Hugh looked casual tonight with a woollen jumper on with jeans and brown leather boots. We had a couple of pints and talked about the usual stuff, how was work and home, etc., and then Hugh said, "come on, let's get out of here." "Where are we going," I asked, "I've just got to meet a mate of mine in Telford, we won't belong." We had a quick cigarette in the car park and then got back into his Porsche.

Quickly heading off in the direction of Telford, he put his foot down after leaving the speed restriction zone, and my body was thrust into the back of the seat. "Oh my god," "What a fantastic car this is, and it sounds beautiful" I said, as we went into hyperdrive down the straights hurtling towards our destination.

Arriving in a housing estate, Hugh started to drive slowly, looking at the street names until finally coming to a stop at the side of a road. A man looking out of the window stepped out of his house and walked towards us. Hugh got out his car and closed the door, walking to meet this man, who I presumed was his mate. Hugh was standing with his back to me, and the guy was in front of him; they talked for only a minute or so, before Hugh turned, walking back, got back into his car. "That was quick I said," as Hugh smiled. He was acting a bit funny and kept looking around for some reason, but I just thought he was concerned about his car as this estate did look a bit rough.

We drove off, and shortly Hugh stopped at a corner shop and said he wouldn't be a minute as he entered the shop. A minute or two after, getting back into his car and saying: "Right, that's it lets go." "Where are we going now, Hugh?" "We will head over to see another mate I have around here; it's just up the road." Shortly after, we pulled up to a section of flats that looked very run down, and I was surprised Hugh wanted to go to see someone who lived here, but I didn't want to judge, so I kept quiet as we approached the door and Hugh buzzed the intercom with an unusual Morse code pattern. The door buzzed open, and we entered a hard landing with concrete stairs and graffiti on the walls. Taking two flights of stairs, I was thinking God, this is a right shit hole as we stopped, and Hugh knocked on a door.

Opening to reveal a skinny guy, dirty looking who nervously asked us in. The flat smelt terrible, a combination of damp and body odour. It had a couch, a table, a coffee table, and a bed all in one room. The bed linen looked dirty, and there was a broken window where the dark night was whipping a cold draft through. The rising damp suffocated your senses, and the guy was standing with his arms crossed, trying to keep warm. Hugh started a conversation with him, asking how he was and how he had been, then introduced me, and the guy said Hi. Hugh pulled out a red bull can, opened it up, and drinking the contents in one, and Hugh asked if I would like a cigarette. "No, thanks, I said, I will have a roll-up."

Hugh started to smoke his cigarette while making conversation with this still nervous looking guy. "Have you got a toilet I can use I asked?" "Yes, just round that wall second door." I got up and moved towards the door, opening it to see a bed with a girl asleep half-naked. "Shit" as I quickly closed the door, she didn't wake up, and I was pleased I hadn't disturbed her, she was a slim girl with shoulder-length blonde hair lying face down on the bed wearing only a pair of purple coloured underwear on.

Locating the toilet, which was the third door down, I took a piss and returned into the front room, not saying anything about what I had seen. Hugh was messing with the red bull can, and denting it, while he flicked his ash on the table, which I thought was kind of rude. Then Hugh started piercing the can with a needle that he had. "What the hell are you doing?" I asked, "Laughing, oh, you'll see in a minute," as he then scraped some of the cigarette ash off the table onto the end of his red bull can. I have no idea what the hell he's doing, I thought but continued to watch with curiosity. Hugh then pulled out a wrapper from his pocket and opened it on the table.

I could not see what he was doing as I was sitting on the couch across the room, but I had a clear view. Hugh was messing with something in his fingers and placing something on the ash on the red bull can. Holding the can up to his mouth with the drinking side open end by his mouth, Hugh got his lighter and burned the ash, whilst it appeared to spark and crackle with Hugh inhaling what seemed to be a colossal drag.

Hugh looking like he was going to burst, exhaled fast, then slowly as he let out the remaining fumes. What is he doing, I thought? Hugh looked like he had gone a bit dizzy as he held onto the table, and his eyes widened bigger than I had ever seen before, starting to breathe in and out like he was trying to control himself. Hugh panting, remained holding onto the table for some time, head down catching his breath, then smiling the biggest smile, while giggling. Breaking something in his fingers, Hugh then repeated the process, putting more ash from off the table back onto the can and past it to the flat guy. This guy did the same and sat down on a chair, passing the pipe back to Hugh. Hugh repeated the process, breaking something in his fingers and placing it at the end of the can.

"Here you are, Malc, come and try this." I stepped towards him and said, "what is it, Hugh?" "don't worry, it's just an upper; it will make you feel great after a drag." "Only light that small white rock with the lighter, take a deep breath and blow out till you have no breath left, then put your mouth on the can whilst lighting the rock and start inhaling, keep it burning until you can see the rock gone, while inhaling it all in one deep breath, hold the breath, as long as you can then let go slowly blowing out the smoke." How bizarre I thought, I've never seen this before, but I'm always happy to try something once, so I did what Hugh said. Holding the mouth part of the can to my lips, blowing a deep breath out as instructed by Hugh, I lighted the rock with the lighter. Then started to take a deep breath slowly but consistently until the stone appeared to be all gone with the fumes now in my lungs. I held as much as I could and released quickly. What happened next took me by complete surprise.

Every cell in my body appeared to orgasm, the euphoria was insane, the feeling of complete happiness washed over me instantly like a cleansing from God, all my aches and pains were gone in a second. The sexual rush throughout the whole of my body was the best feeling I have ever felt. Then came the heavy breathing, lightheadedness, where I felt like I was going to be sick or pass out. Taking deep breaths in and out, I continued like this for about three minutes, trying not to be sick, trying not to faint. Once this rush had passed, I was in heaven, pure, undiluted ecstasy beyond that of any words can justify. It was insane, but I loved it, and I felt amazing!

Hugh's face looked like there were five invisible hands just tickling his body all over with one hand where it shouldn't have been, his eyes were wide, and his head wobbled slightly from side to side. His back arched, and his elbows on his knees just sitting in a coma of pleasure with sporadic outbursts of giggles. The other guy sat in a chair with the same expression, no longer shivering due to the cold and contempt in his own little world of ecstasy. Time stopped still as a feeling of being in-between time, and reality washed over me. Hugh started to arrange another go, and my eyes opened more comprehensively, with my heart racing in the eager anticipation of another go. It is almost like being teased by a lap dancer and then being beckoned behind a curtain or starving and watching someone prepare and cook a ten-ounce rump of fillet steak and be passed a knife and fork.

The anticipation was killing me, my hands started to shake and my fingers tensed as I gripped the arm of the couch, moving myself to the edge of the sofa and sitting upright in begging style as I homed in on the action of Hugh as he placed a large white rock on the end of the can pipe. A raging hunger raced through my body, where every cell appeared to scream like a vampire craving the blood of a young virgin. An animal nature had overtaken my usual placid demeanour, and nothing mattered in the whole world apart from the need for just one more pipe. My body trembled from the constant feeling of a thousand orgasms cascading one after the other, endless, eternal.

Hugh drew in his breath to inhale this one carrot lump of euphoria, and I found myself thinking me next, please me next! Patience was not something that came quickly, and my breathing started to get cumbersome and faster. Hurry up, Hugh, promptly pass it on, I thought! Next, following the routine was this guy's turn. Dam! I thought, as my fingernails were digging into the couch, must I wait much longer? My eyes trained on the guy as he quickly got into his inhale. Yes, Yes, hurry, my turn now, pass it on I screamed silently in my head. As he passed me the can pipe, Hugh stood up and attempted to walk over to me on the couch, holding something in his fingers. As he approached, he said, this is a special one for you, Malc. A large chunk of shiny white rock, the size of a sweetcorn kernel. "Here you are, Malc, that will be f****g amazing mate Hugh said." Slowing right down in my movements not wanting to drop this nugget of pure pleasure, I took the lighter from Hugh in my right hand and slowly raised the pipe with the cigarette ash and the rock in my left hand towards my lips. First, taking in the deepest breath, I could and slowly blowing out. Raising it firmly in a sucking position, I lit the lighter. The rock started to sizzle as I slowly inhaled, watching it burn and get smaller and smaller, still inhaling deeper as the whole rock disappeared and became a part of my essence. The aluminium taste was prominent, and the smell was indescribable as I held my breath with it deep in my lungs for a record time, before my lungs thrust it back out of my lips in a disco smoke machine style. My body instantly flew back into a slouching position on the couch, which now felt like a seat between two massive warm breasts. What a hit, I thought as I started to go up, my breathing getting faster as I loudly panted in and out. "Don't be sick" shouted Hugh, my head was spinning any second now I felt I would pass out. "Deep, slow breaths Malc," cried, Hugh. The internal struggle was immense, almost like my body was clawing from the inside, trying to get out. Then, like a big dipper, I had reached the top. It plateaued for one second and started to decline, and that's where the ecstasy train hit me smack right in the face, gushing down my complete body into every finger and toe. An invisible high-powered vibrator pressing down hard on my G-spot sent sexual voltage to my groin area, which smashed throughout my body like a meteor crashing into earth and exploding hot fiery rock into a million pieces throughout my veins and nerves. That moment of coming off that peak was beyond words; it was a feeling not of this world.

After some time, past, as we all sat in this place that felt like we were wrapped in a duvet of love and ecstasy, I started talking to the guy whose place it was. His name was Peter, we got talking for a while, and Peter volunteered his story to me.

"I had been working as a painter and decorator and was living with my girlfriend and two-year-old daughter Melissa." "Things were good for six months but started to go wrong when they were struggling to pay the bills." "Arguments began, and then came the drinking, which led to more arguments, and finally, my girlfriend asked me to leave." "I didn't have any family as both my parents had died, and I ended up in a homeless shelter as the council would not give me a place." He said, because I was not fleeing a war-torn country, I was not a danger to myself or others, I was not just getting out of prison, and I didn't suffer from mental health or was the disabled." "Waiting time for a flat could be eighteen years." "I had no choice but to go into a shelter, which also meant losing my job as I had to change areas due to available space." He continued to say, "my ex was stopping me seeing Melissa, and as I had no home now, my ex would not let me have her on the weekends and deemed where I was living, dangerous for her to go to. Months past and I started getting depressed." "No one can understand how deeply traumatic it is to lose your soul mate and be separated from your daughter you love so much." "One day, my mate in the hostel offered me some drugs, and it gave me a small window of time to forget my own pain and sadness." "Now I will never see my daughter again, but the pain will stop soon."

Hugh shouted over," Hey! You don't want to be bloody doing that, I've told you before, you'll be alright, things will work out." Peter crouched in his chair, looking at Hugh, nodding as his knees bounced up and down with his arms crossed. I could see the sorrow so deep within him, and I could feel my eyes filling up with tears. In the drug-fueled state that I was, I felt incompetent to be able to offer Peter any words to lift him, but there, as I looked at him, I could hear the silent scream coming from his anguish, and I wondered what a hug from his daughter could do for his spirit. Obviously, he would need to get clean, but it seems no one will throw him a crumb of hope to motivate him to walk that path.

It was time to leave now, and Peter's story left a sadness in my heart as I went and shook his hand, leaving him in this cold, damp flat that had become his Thailand cell. As I walked with Hugh down the stairs, I thought to myself, he would be better off in prison, at least he would have people to talk to, heating and hot food.

I felt Peter was a horrible example of what can happen when love turns wrong.

It seems we had been at Peters a long time, and it looked early hours in the morning as we entered Hugh's lovely car, setting off to go home. I was starting to feel normal again but had this broken shivering feeling, as I would talk, I would be jumping around in my seat and feeling twitchy, agitated almost. Hugh looked over and said, don't worry, we will stop soon, shortly after pulling into a layby on a dark outskirt's road, he pulled out tin foil from his glove compartment. "What are you going to do with that Hugh?" "cook some chicken?" Laughing loudly. "No, you will see, this will help your irritable feeling as he unwrapped some brown powder held in a paper style envelope, folding the foil, and making a line. "I have no idea what you are doing, Hugh?" Hugh just smiled and said, "you will see, you will feel better after this."

Taking out a pen from his pocket and removing the insides, he jostled in his seat to manoeuvre himself into position and held the foil up to his chin with the plastic tube to his mouth. Lighting the bottom of the tin foil, Hugh inhaled the vapour from the sizzling powder, which instantly smelt disgusting. "Here you are, Malc, try this," as Hugh past the foil and the lighter. Feeling like I was going to say no second, I hesitantly took it off Hugh and said, "I don't know if I want to, but I will try a little bit." Repeating the process, I lit the foil and inhaled through the tube, which lasted only a few seconds before I stopped. "That's disgusting," as I blew out the one drag giving it back to Hugh. "You will want to have more than that Malc, have at least another significant breath." "Okay, Hugh, but just one, its f****g horrible." Lighting the foil one more time and watching the burning vapour's rise, I inhaled a considerable drag over five seconds, passing it instantly to Hugh, choking and blowing out the nasty fumes. "That is truly horrible!" Hugh smiled, "yes, but it will do you good and help you settle and relax."

Moments later, I started to feel strange, like someone had spiked my drink. My vision was blurred, my breathing was slowing, and my head just rested against the passenger window, my cheek pressing against the glass, my eyes rolling as Hugh started the car. Slurring my words like I was very drunk, I asked Hugh, "are you okay to drive?" "Oh, I'm fine Malc, I'm too used to it, that was nothing for me" as he accelerated out of the layby. My face still pressing on the window like I was tranquillized and couldn't move. The car hurtled in the direction of home, with my eyes barely opened, looking at the darkness of the night with the background noise of a racing Porsche.

The streetlights jumped around as the car got up to a blistering speed, everything seemed to slow down to an almost stop. My eyes could see the now glowing continuous line of the streetlights, and any moment soon, we were going to crash, and I was going to die, I thought. The streetlights became my very own flatline. I hoped it would be instant and that I would not feel any pain. I didn't feel anyone would care when it happened, and, at that moment, I held my hands out to death to take me, closing my eyes and ready to embrace death any second now, waiting for it second by second for impact.

"Malc, Malc, wake up, we are back home now, go get back in your house" Hugh shouted. I sat up and struggled to open my eyes, "where are we?" "Home, outside your house." "Its 4am time for you to go to bed." We made it; we didn't crash, I thought. It was a nice feeling to be home as I shook Hugh's hand and crawled out of the car, walking like some type of spaceman unable to use my legs correctly. Opening the door and entering my front room, falling on to the couch instantly. What a fucked-up night!

The next day I woke feeling like death, staggering to the bathroom for a shower to wash off the nightmare of last night. What was I thinking? How could I be so stupid? Never again, I thought.

Chainsaw Attack

At work, it was hard to enter communication with people as I felt that inside, I feared it would be evident in my language and expressions that something was wrong with me. Coming into the café upstairs for a full English breakfast and copious amounts of coffee, I tried to heal myself with food, which did make me feel much better. Two o'clock came round quickly and an urgent call over my radio asking directly for my assistance: "Mike Three to Charley One, IC1 male in store selecting items and approaching doors, can you assist, please?" Blimey, that's next door, I thought as I ran towards the high street doors. "Charley One to Mike Three, what's his description" as I pushed through the double glass door into the high street. "Mike Three to Charley One green jacket, blonde hair, stolen a jumper, it's in his coat." Out Mike Three's door came to a lad fitting the description, taking one look at me, he starts to run, as I turned and took chase.

"Delta Two to Charley One, we've got the cameras on you now Toby echoed" as I'm into a full sprint after this lad. Gosh, he can run I thought, he is going like a bat out of hell towards the roundabout, then right into a dual carriageway with very fast-moving cars. Turning a second or two after him, I observed he had run into the road and ran up the central line in between the oncoming traffic. Timing it successfully, I followed, both of us at full sprint running towards the vehicles as they were passing in two lanes. One car had several people in, and one man shouted. "Get him Malc" as my eyes glanced him quickly, I noticed it was a car full of police officers but I had no time to chat, I was on fire, and I was gaining distance closing in on him. Switching to the side of the double lane, the lad accelerated more while occasionally looking back to see if I was still in pursuit. My speed was unusually quick, and my adrenaline was supercharged as he started to slow, and with one last push of momentum, I held the back of his jacket. Slowing and twisting trying to get away, we had reached a path where I dragged him onto and secured an instant arm lock bending him over my right leg. "Alright! You've got me, let me go." He shouted, he was exhausted and breathing heavily, finding it hard to speak. "Okay, I told him, keep it calm, keep your hands out of your pockets as I will see it as an act of aggression, we will walk back together briskly and have you banned from that store, give me the jumper." He took it out of his trousers where he had tucked it in for the getaway sprint, and we carried on calmly walking back to the store. My left hand on his left wrist and my right hand on his left elbow, ready to reverse turn into a lock-in case he started to kick off, which I'm pleased he chose not too as he was a big lad and could have easily given me some trouble.

Back through the store doors, I took him to their backroom while we waited for the police and Brian who was the store detective. filling out the forms, everything went smoothly, and very soon, he was arrested and in cuffs being led away. Brian and the store manager thanked me and offered a 50% discount in return for my help, where I smiled and said "thank you," although it's not the kind of shop I would buy clothes from, the kind thought was there.

By now, it was almost four o'clock in the afternoon, and I made my way back to the loading bay for a cigarette and a coffee. It was dark and bitterly cold, Christmas shoppers struggled with multiple bags of gifts as they rushed from shop to shop trying to get it done as fast as possible. I believed my day would end without further problems until Mike One shouted up on the radio: "Delta Two, two IC1 males leaving my store now and heading up Bartlett street." "Yes, yes Mike One, we've picked them up, what have they been up too?" "Mike One to Delta Two, I believe one has something in his jacket." "Delta Two to Mike One, okay, I will monitor them and see if they pull anything out." "Mike One to Delta Two, thank you for that, I didn't see them select but there acting suspiciously."

Turning my radio down as they were about to walk right past me at the loading bay, I observed one lad looking back at Mike One's location, then turning around and laughing to his mate, while pulling a blue jumper from inside his coat in clear view at the top of his zip. They walked past and turning up my radio, I called Delta Two to say I was going to do a stop as I believed I had seen the stolen item in one of the lad's jackets. Delta Two confirmed they were monitoring as I stepped out of the loading bay fifteen feet behind them.

Seconds later, one lad turned, spotted me, and both bolted running towards the corner end of the town, which encompassed a park.

Now we are in a full sprint again, dodging customers and running over roads, jumping small fences, and crossing car parks, over roundabouts, and dangerously coming close to traffic. I pursued them to the side of the river at the bottom of a small car park.

I thought there's nowhere to go now as I was about ten feet behind moving in quickly. Then splash! They had jumped in the river to get away from me. As I got to the bank, I could see them now paddling through the middle of the freezing cold river towards the muddy bank. There was no way I could run all the way to the nearest bridge to cross as it was too far away. There was only one action left, go in after them!

Taking a short run in the opposite direction, I turned, looked at the river and my run-up, thinking in my head (you're a f*****g idiot Malc) I ran full speed towards the bank, I could see one lad had made it to the other side. Still, one lad was struggling three quarters way across, but now was no time for changing my mind as I landed with my last right foot long jumping three parts way across before almost landing on the other lad as he shit himself as I splashed into the river right on top of him. The cold was shocking, like a million needles piercing my body, but my Army side said, just get on with it and ignore the discomfort. Grabbing him by his collar, I swam, pulling him the short distance to the bottom of the bank. He was in trouble and was losing his strength. As it turns out, his mate had climbed out and run off into the darkness. The bank was steep and muddy, as we struggled to get out of the freezing water. I was able to pull myself out, swinging my legs onto the bank and rolling out while leaning down and offering a hand for this lad to get out of the bitterly cold water. Eventually, we were both out panting on the side of the bank, with him shivering and complaining the cold was painful. Putting my training into action, I knew we needed to get in the warm and dry as soon as possible, and most importantly, increase our body temperature. After briefly explaining this, we started to jog in our soaking wet clothes back into the town towards the location of my store. My radio was knackered and running with one hand on his arm with saturated wet cloths and squelching combat boots was awkward enough.

Back in the store, we headed straight for my office and the lost property box, where we managed to change into warm and dry jumpers and tracksuit tops, although annoyingly, no one had lost trousers, so it was the radiator or nothing.

Of course, the two jumpers that had been stolen were ruined, but the successful theft had been thwarted and one male detained. Calling CCTV on the landline, I arranged for the police to come to collect this male, who volunteered his name as John, twenty-eight from Manchester. Apparently, John was stealing the jumpers to get a train ticket back as he, and his mate had drunk their fare in a bar in Birmingham that day and only had money to get halfway home.

The police were quick to attend, where John was swiftly arrested and taken to the station with one officer staying with me to write a statement. I remember the officer looking at me, once I explained what had happened with a look of sheer confused expression as to why I would jump into the river on this cold winter afternoon for the sake of two jumpers. However, it was not about the two jumpers; it was an enemy trying to getaway. Today it was two jumpers, tomorrow, it could be someone's purse or a teenage girl's mobile phone; either way, it was a theft that I had the opportunity to stop. Also, they jumped in the river because I was chasing them, if John had drowned, it might have been on me, so assisting him out of the river was a kind of duty of care, I guess. Being ex-army, they used to make us do river crossings in full kit all the time, especially at 5am on the first march, just to harden us up, so it was nothing unusual for me.

I couldn't wait to get the car heater on that night, as my soaking trousers clung to my legs on the short brisk walk to the car park. Driving with the discomfort of wet clothes was shit, but as the thoughts developed in my mind, the overpowering feeling of fuck em rang through my mind. Although I did wonder what had happened to his mate, soaking wet, trying to get back to Manchester. I guess he would have just locked himself in the toilet on the train until reaching his home station.

After a boiling bath, a hot meal at home and a short spell of trying to be a good dad to my kids, I hit the bar for a casual few pint. Hoping not to see Hugh after our last night out. The bar was dead but had a roaring open fire, which I gladly sat almost on top of as I contemplated the day I had just had.

My body ached, and as I sat on my stool with my head looking to the floor holding my pint, I thought to myself, what am I doing to myself? This constant worry and stress, the fear for my own life on occasion, little thanks and six pounds eighty an hour, I must be crazy, surely? But then I remembered Whiskey Kilo, the event, the trigger, my shock, trauma, sadness, and depression. Suck it up Malc, I thought! I must be making progress. I had to believe I was making a difference, even just a small one.

The following day I had a phone call from my head office as a fellow guard had communicated my river crossing to a supervisor at my base. After explaining the incident, my supervisor offered me a transfer to a store for three weeks that was experiencing high theft and assaults on the current guard. It was in a location no one wanted to work in. A site that was notoriously bad for the crime on the outskirts of Birmingham. It carried a pay increase for the three weeks, while the current guard was off sick due to being assaulted at the site. A relief guard would replace me at my store, and I agreed to go in three days.

That evening I was back in the gym with my full dose of supplements, smashing a three-hour work out then a four-mile run back to my village arriving home just before my kids were going to bed. I did wonder what I had signed myself up for, knowing this place and the reputation it had. Three days past uneventful and tomorrow I would leave.

On the train going through the outskirts of Birmingham, I looked out the window at some of the buildings, canals, derelict factories, and I instantly thought, this place is a shit hole. Shortly afterwards, I quickly found myself heading to this well-known store, where I was sure that things were about to get real.

Walking into the store on my first day, a manager greeted me and said: "Are you a hard bastard?" "Because you'll need to be here, it's like the Bronx." Responding, I just said, "I can look after myself, don't worry about me." I asked him "where is my radio, and what is CCTV call sign to sign in." "No radio or CCTV here, mate, he said," "You're on your own."

Great! No backup, no cameras, no help, what the f**k have I walked into? I thought. It was a DIY store, cold and vast, with high isles making selection and concealment easy, so I chose to stand at the front double doors to observe customers coming in and out, looking for the apparent types, who generally would try to act normal. They simply couldn't resist giving me evil looks as they entered, which was always a red flag.

Day one went quickly, some real nut cases had come in, but I seemed to spoil their plans as I hovered in their chosen isle in plain view. I got told to "f**k off" a few times, but I said I am just doing my job. If there was a distinct look of an ex-prisoner, I must have seen easily thirty on my first day, all looking like they had been bought up in hell and looking around for cameras with large oversized jackets on. This first day, I didn't see any proven theft.

Day two started well with the sun shining and a couple of coffees before I began my shift while talking to the staff's manager. "Well, no thefts yesterday," I said. "They were just weighing you up," he said, "look out the next couple of days." His words did make me uneasy, to be honest, there were some right hard-looking individuals yesterday casing the store, but I was confident that when shit hit the fan, I would feel at home.

Just after lunch shit hit the fan as two IC1 males left the store with two expensive drills and a garden leaf blower, in their hands without going through the tills and no sold tape on the items. They were ten steps into the car park when I grabbed hold of the first guy, who was six feet three, medium to stocky build carrying the drills.

To say he kicked off would be the understatement of the year. Within two seconds, I was in a full-blown fight with him. He was determined to chop me down to the floor with a psychotic barrage of punches to my head with his full power, while his mate was booting me in my arse. I was in imminent danger of severe injury and alone with these two head cases. Shielding my head with my arms, trying to stop the blows from making contact with my skull, still being booted in my arse, I looked down under my guard and side kicked in a downward motion his right knee in a no holds barred attempt to break his leg. One punch can kill a man, I've seen it, so fuck em I thought. He hit the floor, screaming as his mate now jumped on my back in a stranglehold and pulled me backwards in a bent position, as he strangled me to the concrete. Noticing his hand grip quickly with a thumb not curled into his grip, I grabbed his thumb and attempted to snap it clear off his hand as he screamed like the little bitch he was.

Free from the stranglehold, his mate was still on the car park tarmac; I launched forward at his mate, putting him in a reverse arm lock and face down onto the ground. His mate now, trying to kick me in the face. Still, no one from the store had come out, no one to help or call the police, no radio or CCTV, and these guys were big and strong, and I was starting to get exhausted. One other kick contacted my face and sent me hurtling towards the tarmac but still holding the other lads lock. At that point, I felt stunned and somewhat in shock as my ears started to ring, and I became faint.

Raising my arm as he swung the next kick, I lifted his leg into the air throwing his balance off and having him flat on his back next to me, with a quick neck chop to disable him, I instantly threw my weight on top of him. moving my restraining lock on his mate to a scissor lock with my legs around his throat.

Seconds later, as they pulled away in opposite directions, they were free and standing up after applying all their strength, but I still had his mates' arm as we tumbled back to the floor, hitting the ground hard. The other lad ran off towards a red Astra, while I applied pressure into another arm lock while I still had his mate, which we were now flat on the floor, him still resisting.

Then I heard the horrifying sound. A sound of anyone's nightmares. A chainsaw starting up, as his mate had taken it from the boot of his car. F**k me! I thought these guys are f****g crazy! I had now quickly found a sudden surge of strength as I manoeuvred his mate, still in an armlock to a sitting position facing his mate, who was now running at me with the petrol stream of smoke billowing out of the screaming engine. Using his mate as a shield, I shrunk behind him in a crouched position making sure I could manoeuvre him like a puppet and acting as a screen with my other hand gripping his hair. "Put that fucking back now", his detained mate shouted. The sound of the swinging chainsaw was horrifying, and I was bloody frightened, I mean, incredibly f****g scared as he attempted to swing at my head and manoeuvre around to my back. Any minute now, I could be fucked, I thought. Which was even more reason to keep his mate as a screen; without him, I would be completely exposed. His detained mate screamed one more time to put it back, and the lad ran back to his car with the chainsaw turning it off as he approached the open boot, where he slammed it shut, getting into the car and starting it up.

Revving it high, he accelerated towards us as again as I continued to use his mate as a shield, hoping he wouldn't run over his mate. The car started to circle us as I kept his mate spinning to block his mate's opportunity of hitting me with the vehicle. Then his mate, who I had in the arm lock, started to elbow me in the face with his other arm, and on the third or fourth strike, I felt like I was about to be knocked out, and at that moment, I let him go.

He ran limping to the car, while his mate had to wait for him to get in the passenger door. With both in the car now, it turned quickly in my direction. I had been punched, kicked, elbowed, and headbutted too many times to remember, and I was critically injured. My vision was blurred, I felt concussed, my legs were bruised all over, and so many other injuries, all I could do was crawl under a purple car parked by me in the car park. I could hear the car getting closer to me as they chased after me, but then with squealing tires, they swung round in a sharp turn to speed off towards the exit of the car park.

The leaf blower and the drills were scattered over the car park, so I collected them and limped back into the store. I was in a real mess, my shirt and trousers were torn, my arms were cut, my back badly bruised from the kicks, my head was bruised all over, I felt sick and tried not to throw up. Then, a guy who worked in the store came running out and said, "where are they?" I said, "they've got away," where he said, "well, you are f****g useless, aren't you?" I had no response to this comment as I limped through the doors with the stolen items, placing them on the customer services desk and making my way up to the washroom.

In the washroom, I took off my shirt and pulled down my trousers to my boots to see the extent of my injuries. F****g hell! It was not good. I had grazed gravel burns over several parts of my body, including my legs, knuckles, elbows, and thighs. I had pain in both legs, bruised ribs, shoulder pain, a right cut eyebrow, and a split bottom lip. I needed to go to the hospital, but that would have left the store without a guard for two more hours. So I decided to suck it up and adopt an aggressive attitude of shut the f**k up Campbell and just get on with it, as my corporal would often say in the middle of a nine-mile forced march.

After putting a call into the police and waiting with no attendance, I decided to finish my shift as the store closed and head for the train station.

Arriving at the bus stop, a short walk from the store was a nervous moment; every car passing had my heart pounding, wondering if the lads from earlier would come back to take their revenge. After all, they too must have taken some injuries, but tonight it would appear, I was to be lucky.

Getting on the train, finding a seat was a relief as my body throbbed with pain from my knees to my head. The thought of finishing off my assignment at this store left me with a sick feeling in my gut. What would happen tomorrow? Or the next day? It seemed to me that any day now I could get stabbed. My emotions on the train home were mixed; on the one aspect, I was pleased I had prevented the theft and showed them that I was no pushover, but for what cost? It was more than just avoiding theft in my mind, it was good against evil, standing up for what's right. I was upset they had got away, but I also felt somewhat lucky to get away with only the injuries I had sustained.

With my head against the steamed-up window filtering the tracks' vibration into my body through the dark night, allowing house lights to occasionally break the veil of the shadows, I felt so sad and lonely. My nervous system was taxed as I could see my hands shaking, and I had an overwhelming feeling that I was about to cry, and aware that I was fighting hard to hold it back as my eyes filled up with tears.

As I closed my eyes, I imagined the beautiful smiling eyes and dark pink voluptuous lips of a pretty young lady kissing my cheek. Wrapping her arms tight around me, squeezing hard and whispering, "It will be okay, don't worry." For five seconds, my misery and pain disappeared as my mind created an image into a fantasy of hope and love, but five seconds were not long enough, I needed a five-hour hug like this. I had a concussion.

Arriving home and putting on a happy persona as I entered the front room saying hi to my wife and kids, giving my children a big hug, I made my way upstairs to have a long soak in the bath. Trying not to scream out as the hot water submerged my beaten body with my eyes as big as saucers and my breath panting to somewhat ease the experience of only having a bath. It was ridiculous.

While I lay there eventually feeling calm and relaxed, I understood I needed to talk to someone. I couldn't speak to my wife, as we were not on those terms anymore and I also would not want to cause her concern for me as she had a hard-enough job looking after three kids on her own.

People in the pub don't want to talk about deep and personal stuff. They go there to get away from things like that. Not having anyone to talk too is a horrible and lonely aspect that I knew was causing my well-being considerable damage. I felt I was going down in my own mind. I was sure I was starting to feel unstable and after my bath decided I needed to get out of the house for fear of a conversation that might end up with me crying in front of my wife and kids.

Now 9pm, the pub's distraction and being surrounded by other people was the best I could hope for, so I quickly got dressed and told my wife I was popping out for a quick pint.

It was a slow walk to the pub as I was still in pain and entering the warm atmosphere of a burning log fire and laughter, was just what I needed. It seemed everyone's world was better than mine as I saw them chat and laugh at the bar as I started on my first pint.

How far away all these people are, from the day that I have had, I thought, living life in their own bubble. Although I secretly envied them. Sitting quietly with the occasional fake smile, so I didn't look depressed, I wondered if I was killed at work one day, would I be missed? Would anyone here raise a beer for me? But that's the life I thought, and the only thing I can do is try to make a difference tomorrow and the next day. After listening to my own thoughts, I cheered up and quickly sank another pint, starting to get into a conversation with some people I knew. Nigel and Hugh were not in tonight, so it was joining in with the crowd.

It turned out that it ended a good night, and it was just what I needed to take my mind off the fact that I was back at that place the next day. It was now 22.50, and I was halfway through my final beer after having maybe five, when two lads walked in and approached the bar.

They were both in their early twenties about 5ft 11inches, white males, thin and gaunt looking. Instantly, I thought they were not from the village, and they had the look of many people I come across within my job. I felt uneasy in their aura and decided to move over by the fire. The landlord rang the bell for last orders, and they ordered their beers. I was thinking of leaving, but I could almost smell trouble from these guys, and the pub was quarter full of older ladies and gentlemen in their senior years. I thought maybe it's just me being judgmental, and I hovered back by the fire waiting for them to leave. After finishing their beer, they shouted over to the landlord for another pint, to which he said, sorry, last orders have been called, and we have stopped serving now. "Just pour me a f****g pint." Shouted one of them. Oh, shit, I thought, here we go, I knew they were trouble. The landlord cried over, "time for you guys to leave now, we don't have swearing in this place."

The other customers were starting to get their coats as they sensed things were about to kick off. The landlord was by the bar hatch opposite the fire, the two lads were around the corner of the bar by the front door. After hearing what the landlord had said, one lad barged round the bar to confront him at the hatch and knocked this elderly woman over into a round small bar table, where she fell, knocking the empty glasses onto the floor. In his late seventies, her husband quickly went to her rescue. While this lad became almost level with the hatch where the landlord was standing. Arguing with him and pointing his finger aggressively at the landlord shouting at him, I looked across to see where his mate was, and he had disappeared.

Within seconds, I was thinking, where is he? Has he gone to a car to get a weapon? By this time, the pub had almost emptied with people hurrying out the door, leaving me and the landlord and three women sitting around in the lounge area. This could turn into something nasty I thought. They have endangered members of the public and are now acting in a threatening manner with one lad worryingly not insight. The landlord was trying to get a word into the conversation with little success as this lad carried on arguing and pointing his finger in the landlord's face. At that point, I thought now was the time to try to prevent this from getting into an uncontrollable situation. Right or wrong, I was stepping in. Jumping forward to him as he had his back towards me and grabbing the top of his left arm with my right hand and his left wrist with my left wrist, instantly twisting and bending him into a restraint position over my right leg. His right arm was now on the floor, preventing him from ending up on the floor, I shouted to the landlord to get the front door. Manoeuvring this lad in a full arm lock and in a crouched position towards the front door, while the landlord held the door open.

Obviously, this lad was trying to kick off, swearing and threatening to kill me once he got free, which was the ordinary, everyday shit I would here. He was incapacitated in the shoulder and arm lock, pushing his shoulder down towards the floor. Still, he was giving it all the best prison style of threats that he could, hoping that I would release him, which I did, as I almost threw him out of the door as the landlord locked it, bolting it three times. I told him to call the police, and as he did, I checked the toilets to see if his mate was hiding in there, which thankfully he was not.

I was aware of my actions and thought genuinely about the lads' rights I had removed from the pub, but I felt at some point that I would have to make the call, the decision to act, in the interest of safety for the landlord, the ladies and myself. It wasn't about being a gung-ho hero, that couldn't be furthest from the truth. It was about sensing things that were about to escalate into violence. My decision to step in and take control of the situation was simply an attempt to prevent the course of action that I believed the lad was set on making. Sometimes someone must intervein and act in the hope that action prevents injury.

After some time passed, the landlord let me out the side door. The police still hadn't arrived, and the ladies wanted to stay until they arrived. I said to the landlord, I would be available for a statement if they needed one tomorrow. I cautiously walked home, ensuring I didn't walk close to hedges or parked cars in case they were waiting for me. I was worried and obviously nervous, but I was on full alert, looking around always as I walked the long route home to make sure I was not followed, and the location of my house was revealed.

The rest of my assignment at this DIY store passed without too much drama. I successfully prevented several more thefts by being a visual deterrent, got told to f**k off maybe fifty more times but none of these incidents escalated into anything of notability at work, and I left thinking what a shit hole of a store to be a permanent guard.

Hit and Run

I was pleased to get back into my regular store within my hometown, and I suddenly felt that I had never left. Calling the CCTV room and catching up with who is active, and what I had missed bringing me up to speed with the current situation.

The girls in the store were happy to see me. Each section filled me in on what if anything had been going on or stolen. Two girls were particularly showing the excitement of my return. I was very flattered with their beautiful smiles and gooey eyes as they hovered near towards me, smelling like strawberries and roses with their shinny long virgin hair. Just talking to them would get my heart racing and make my normally fluent speech turn into a shy, stuttering teenage boy trying to act cool around the gorgeous head girls at school. They were both angels, and I could only fantasize about having someone so beautiful as they were on my arm.

It was funny because I was older than them, but their presence would make me go to bits inside. It's strange though, I thought, that I may have the courage to do the things I do, but when in front of a gorgeous girl, I'm as much use as a chocolate fireguard.

Later after lunchtime, Oscar Two shouted up on the radio for aid, which I quickly responded to as they were only two stores up. Not knowing what I was walking into, my heart was racing a little, and I was primed for action as I entered the store to see a gentleman of Chinese ethnicity standing at the counter with the rest of the store empty. Standing back, I observed from the window, as this gentleman gathered five bags together and started to walk out of the store. Calling CCTV, I got the cameras to follow him as I approached the salesperson to find out what the problem was. After some checks on the telephone, the sales assistant had confirmed that the credit card used to buy eight hundred pounds of goods was a clone card, and now this gentleman was guilty of credit card fraud and, therefore, theft of eight hundred pounds of stock.

Just as I flew out of the door in pursuit of this male asking CCTV to give me his location, a police officer joined me. He was 6ft 2inch, stocky build with all sorts of things weighing him down on his belt. As we both accelerated down raspberry street, I could see him struggling to run, only breaking out of a jog due to his size and equipment he was carrying. I decided to leave him behind as I entered a full sprint through the town. Sprinting around the back of the stores. CCTV had the last location of this male in an area where no cameras were present, and I was to enter this area off-camera and alone. Searching the space up a side street, I heard a noise coming from behind the industrial wheel bins, as I slowly moved in, he jumped out coming straight towards me.

Grabbing him by his jacket, he continued to try to run, until I had little choice but to put him down on the floor using the reverse snake action. (*An act of using your right or left arm only to snake your hand and arm across the front of his neck from one shoulder to the other, then curling your wrist behind his neck pushing back with your arm, bending him backwards, which is dangerous and not a recommended move. But remains an extremely effect one*) Once down, turning him into an arm lock which positioned his body face down on the tarmac, ensuring no injury comes to him and airways are clear. This male was now secure and detained, just as the panting police officer comes running around the corner. Calling him over and placing his cuffs on him, he thanked me and said, I will take it from here! Inside, I laughed to myself and thought, Hey! That was my arrest, I caught and detained him, but I was no police officer, and it was okay that he didn't want to take a statement from me, as he walked back into camera view showing the man under arrest and in cuffs with the five bags of stolen goods. It seemed that would not be the only assistance I would have with the police this day as shortly before 5pm an officer was struggling alone with an arrest in the raspberry street as I observed him through the Royal Dalton section window within my store. This 6ft male was resisting arrest, and the officer was having difficulty on his own as the male was fighting with him. Sprinting out of my store, within a short space of time, with my help, the officer was back in control. The male was face down on the floor and cuffed after another successful snake movement immobilized his resisting behavior. I was so glad to be of help and incredibly happy the officer was able to gain control of the situation. I am always so in awe of the police. They sacrifice and go through so much to protect us all every day. It's brilliant and so courageous in my eyes. This was probably the tenth time I have helped an officer, alone, who was being overpowered, and every time it's been my pleasure, whether I get punched or not.

My security boss asked me for another favour on the phone that day. To go and stand in at a store in Lichfield that was having trouble. The guard was on holiday leave, and the store chose not to replace him. This resulted in a rapid increase in theft, and now the manager wanted someone competent to step in. I was booked for seven days, again in an area I knew nothing about, in a location with no CCTV outside, as the store was a stand-alone store.

This day came around quickly and on my first day, I met with the manager, as he explained his position about his large superstore. My shifts would be 8am till 10pm, and I would be the only security member. No radio, no backup. Story of my life I thought!

My primary role was to be a visual deterrent and patrol close to anyone acting suspiciously. I would take my lunch break for one hour at lunch and half an hour in the afternoon. Three days past with no incidents, but then on days four and five, I was having staff members report several video recorders being stolen. I was flabbergasted, how could this be? I reassured them that I would keep a close eye on them, which was going to be a problem as they had decided to load a whole pallet of them right by the front doors. This meant that if I patrolled the rest of the store, it would leave them vulnerable. I expressed my concern but was overruled and was told it's your job to catch them.

Saturday came quickly, and I was rather glad because it was a long, tedious, uneventful day most days, and Sunday would be my last day.

On my cigarette breaks, I would walk out of the store, turn left and walk to the corner of the store, where there was a path that led around the back of the store, where I would have a quick cigarette and coffee on occasion. Still being given information of video recorders going missing, I pondered while arriving at the back of the store, whether or not I was being watched from the car park by criminals who would dash into the store while I smoked. This time, I took a couple of drags and put it out, swiftly returning towards the front doors of the store.

As I arrived just in front of the doors, the electric double-doors opened to two men who were quickly exiting with arms full of DVD recorders. I had maybe a second to think as they ran straight into me, at which point I put out both of my arms and thrusting my weight forward successfully close lining both men onto the floor in a heap of video recorders. One lad furthest from me got up empty-handed and made a run for the car park, while I through my body on top of the lad that was to my left trying to get up off the floor. It was just my luck that this lad was built like a brick shit house, and I knew I was going to have a hard time alone with this lad, and he did not disappoint me.

We came flying through the double doors exiting the store onto the concrete. Striking me one, two, three times on the side of my head, as I struggled with his strength to secure an arm lock. We must have looked like two Pitbull terriers in a full-blown fight to the death because this guy was muscular, throwing me off him like a rag doll, but instantly I was back onto him. We continued to fight up the five concrete steps and over a knee-high wooden fence into the dirt next to the car park. By now, I was bleeding badly from my nose, lip, and eyebrow, from several punches and a dirty b***d head butt that he caught me with. But I wasn't giving up, and I was keen as ever to nail his arse once he tired a bit. By now, we were into the top quatre of the car park, people were coming and going from the store, but no one wanted to help me, and I could understand why. The sheer strength of this lad was insane, and I was trying to catch a glimpse of his eyes to see if he were on crack, which would have made sense if he were.

After, what seemed about twenty minutes of assault from him, which probably was only ten, I must have been hit with twenty punches to my head, face, stomach and back, I was beginning to lose the will to carry on, but with one last stubborn attempt, I got him in a secure arm lock face down on the car park. For now, he was not going anywhere.

I was worried if he was just resting as he panted with his face pinned to the concrete. Then I heard an unsettling sound of a car engine revving high, as I looked up to see a silver escort screaming towards us on the tarmac. "F**k sake" I shouted" it's his mate! I held onto the lad detained as he stood up, and we both fell over the railing of the trolley park. Hoping his mate would not run us both over, I held onto this lad as he powered closer to the car. I observed as the diesel smoke filled the air along with the sound of squealing tires while circling us with the driver's door close to me. I knew what was coming next as he pushed out the door to hit me. Trying to boot the door shut as he passed, his mate in the car wound down the window, maneuvered out wide, and using his left hand to steer accelerated throwing open his drivers' door to smash into my body as he spun past.

I was now in a terrible way. My ears were ringing, my vision was almost gone, I had gone into shock as I was numb all over with no pain which worried me very much, as this is often the bodies reaction to severe trauma, I could still hear the engine of the car and the squealing of the tires. I had no idea where the other lad had gone, presuming he was now in the car. I vaguely remember getting up sharply, thinking he may try to run me over, and as I managed to stand on both feet, vision blurred, the car hit me again, this time sending me over the wing of the bonnet casting me off to the side of the car as it speeded up towards the exit.

I remember hitting the concrete, I was unsure how long I was lying there by the trolley park, but it was cold, and I was slightly bleeding from my head wound as it felt cold on the back of my head, I had pain everywhere.

Due to the darkness of that part of the car park, I can only presume people didn't see me there. Otherwise, they would have helped.

I got myself to my feet and struggled back to the door. The video recorders were retrieved from the inside of the doors earlier and as I walked in, the customer service attendant said: "Oh my God, do you need an ambulance." It appeared I looked just as bad as I felt. I said "no, my wife will be here in a minute and she will take me to the hospital if I need to go."

My manager at the store was grateful for my actions in saving seven hundred and sixty pounds of stock. As gratitude, he gave me one hundred pounds worth of food vouchers and said he would write a letter of appreciation to my boss, which was more than some stores would have done.

I may have saved the store money and prevented a bulk theft, but I was sure I had lost in my present physical state. I know I got used to being punched when I was younger; however, running over me took the piss.

The adrenaline started to wear off, and I was in agony. Luckily, my wife had needed the car and was due to pick me up at 10pm, which is just as well, as really, I needed to go to the hospital to be honest. I didn't want to scare my kids or my wife by telling them all the details, and I thought I would just monitor myself over the next few hours. Selfishly I suppose, I just wanted a large Jack Daniel's and a hot bath. In the car, I told my wife quietly some of what had happened but kept most of the information to myself due to my children's little ears.

On the way home, we were set to pass my mom's grave at Bretton's churchyard. I asked my wife if she would just stop for a moment while I paid my respects. I knew I would have to climb over the brick wall as it was now 22.30, and the church was closed. I recall sitting by my mom's grave for a few moments, but I don't remember much more than crying. I guess I wished she could see her son acting in a way that was upholding the law rather than fighting and getting into trouble. I suppose secretly, I hoped she was somehow proud of me. Of course, I missed her, but my tears were more telling of my situation, how I felt about my life, and how I couldn't talk to anyone. Deep down, I knew I wouldn't have long left.

Inside, my heart was dying I thought it wouldn't be long before I was reunited with my mom, in fact, I remember clearly my last words as I stood up to go. "See you soon, Mom."

It seemed that when I was high octane in pursuit of criminals, I was at my best, but then after, increasingly lonely, and feeling dead inside. I felt like I was morning a death inside my gut, and I seriously was, it was my own life coming to an end, which my spirit was showing me, and I knew this to be true.

That night in the bathroom, my reaction to my naked reflection in the mirror was memorable as I recall having to put both hands over my mouth tight to stop the sound of crying, continuously flushing the toilet to mask the sounds of my grief. Shocked at how battered, bruised, and cut my entire body was. I couldn't show anyone this, and for the next five nights, I would sleep in tracksuit bottoms and a T-shirt. The next three days I called in sick as I physically couldn't move, and I was feeling deeply depressed. I needed high doses of pain killers to mask the pain from the cuts and muscle bruising.

After hearing from this last store, my bosses had one more job for me to complete before receiving a promotion and making me the new head guard of their biggest spending store in the largest city in the midlands. This store was so prolific, it had its own cells built into the basement due to the high number of thefts, and I was to oversee the team. But before this, I had to go to the hell store.

Notorious amongst us guards as being the worst site known to man for thefts and assaults. Stuck on its own in the middle of a run-down area of Birmingham with two high tower council flat buildings on each side of it surrounded with wasteland and burned-out cars. This place had claimed so many guards' careers after being beaten up, hospitalized, and quitting their jobs. More guards had been put in intensive care at this store than any other Midlands store. Now they were sending me.

I had to travel to Birmingham city centre then get on a bus to the outskirt's location. I was somewhat nervous, to be honest, as it seemed like I was the only outsider in the area. Everyone was looking at me and could clearly see I was not Muslim, and by no fault of my own, I seemed to be attracting considerable attention, which I did not ask for or seek.

Arriving at the store was grim. I could sense the depravity in the air, I could almost smell it. What a f****g shit hole this place was. Everyone looked at me like they wanted to tear my head off. Total hate for my security uniform and everything I stood for. This was not good; I mean incredibly, not right. It felt, smelt, and emanated pure fear and desperation.

Inside the store, there must have been around sixty employees, and I was the only white person.

Three days into my seven-day assignment, no one said a word to me, even though I was there to protect them and their business. Alienated was an understatement here, and soon I was going to find out just how bad things were going to get.

Day four I was patrolling around the alcohol aisle and spotted an IC1 male, aged around fifty, large build, big belly, bald head, select two bottles of whiskey and put them into his black leather jacket, turn and make his way for the entrance door of which he had just come through. Making zero attempts to pay and leaving through the wrong door, I followed him and grabbed hold of his left elbow and wrist, trying to detain him, just as we stepped into the car park. This guy had no intention of stopping for anyone. It all happened in a split second, we hit the floor hard as he took me down. The concrete was wet, stinking of whiskey as the bottles had smashed on impact.

Under-ten seconds later, I had one hand locking his wrist while he was on top of me, brandishing a broken bottleneck of a whiskey bottle in a stabbing action towards my throat. "Holy Shit pressing the panic button on my radio, I'm going to die," I thought, as I managed to get some distance from him while still holding his wrist bending back until he dropped the bottle.

As we continued twisting and rolling, gaining air then slamming back down on the concrete, we eventually found ourselves moving under a parked blue transit van. The male pulled his hand away and reached inside his right outer coat pocket to reveal a small kitchen knife which he was now holding in a full grip with the action of a lower stabbing motion targeting my waist. "Holy Shit" The first thrust missed, as my heart jumped out of my chest, thinking F**k this is it.

I convulsed on the floor to avoid it again, scraping my face on the exhaust and undercarriage of the van. The third thrust got my right boot sole, as he pulled back for thrust number four he was then kicked in the face, which stunned him long enough for me to escape from under the van but not without him slashing my back as a sharp stinging pain ripped through my shirt.

Quickly on to my feet out from one side of the transit, I stepped back towards the store's doors, hoping he would just f**k off.

He did, he ran off through the car park like a raging bull. I had pressed the panic button on my radio just as he started to kick off. This button alerted the internal security members of staff to come out and help me. No one showed up—no one called the police. No CCTV, no backup. I remember being furious as I walked back into the store but kept my mouth shut.

Was it they were too scared to help? Or was it the colour of my skin? I don't know, but sixty people working in a building with a flashing red wall light going off, and no one showed up. Whatever the reason was, I chose not to put energy into that, and after self-patching myself up with the shittest first aid pack available, I continued with my assignment for the remaining few hours. Glad, that I only had three days left.

Through this time, I had the pleasure of speaking to two Muslim ladies in their early twenties. They were beautiful under their black headdress and funny too, I thought they were lovely girls. They told me about their home life with their large family living in one home and what they must do to look after them. I admired their strength and loyalty towards their family. I often wonder if it is just a complete misunderstanding we have with other cultures and they have with us, because once we start talking, we usually both find, we are all lovely people.

After three more grueling days of almost complete silence with no other reports to add, my time was finally up at this store, and I had survived again, but only just!

Heroin Overdose

Saturday night had crept up, and I had collected my bait from the tackle shop in preparation for tomorrow's fishing match. It was 5pm, and I was excited to hit the pub, knowing my bait and tackle was all ready for the 6am departure. After a bath and getting myself looking presentable, I headed to my local for some well-deserved downtime.

Nigel was already looking like he had been there some time, as he was a bit loud and in good spirits. I blended right in and got into my beer quickly as the log fire caressed the country pub atmosphere. Around 8pm, the door swung open, and Hugh stepped through with his usual smart attire with a big smile. I hadn't seen Hugh for a while, and it was nice to see him. Nigel obviously was pissed off to see him, and he turned his back to him. Hugh stood by me and shook my hand, entering the casual chat.

By now, I had consumed about five pints and was relaxed and with good spirits. Hugh stayed close to me and continued to enter a polite conversation with me as we talked about life and how things were going for each of us.

We had gone outside for a cigarette twice and just talked about everyday stuff, but on the third trip outside after I had consumed about eight pints, Hugh asked if I fancied getting out of here for an hour to go up to the other pub by the canal. Not my usual form, but I didn't think there was any harm in it, so I agreed. Saying bye to Nigel receiving an evil look of disapproval as we stepped out of the front door past the car park, thinking we were walking, only to be called over by Hugh to his Porsche. Hugh had consumed three pints of carling and assured me he was fine, although hesitant, I agreed to get into his car in my not so wise eight-pint state as it was only just a two-minute drive. As we approached the pub, Hugh drove past.

Asking Hugh where we were going, he replied he had a better idea, and we would head off to the next city to see someone. "As long as we are not doing anything, I'm fine with that I said" letting Hugh know, I wasn't interested in getting into that shit. Hugh smiled and said, it's alright Malc, relax as he sped off onto the long stretch towards the dual carriageway.

Zipping towards Telford at a blistering speed, Hugh talked to someone on the phone hands-free, but with headphones in, so I was not privileged to the conversation, which I thought was clearly none of my business and took no offence as the engine roared through the gear changes. Slowly approaching a council estate, Hugh said he wanted a red bull, and could I get him one from the corner shop as he pulled up in a parking space with the shop insight. Agreeable and thinking nothing of it, I walked the two minutes to the shop and navigated it until I had found two red bulls, paying, and exiting the shop to walk back to the car. Hugh was sitting in the car with his window open, taking a can off me, and drinking it in one. "Right, let's go, Hugh said." "Where too, now I asked? Just popping round to see a mate for two minutes," he said. Within five minutes, we were outside a block of flats and parking. "Is your car alright here" I asked? "Yeh, everyone knows who I am round here." "It will be fine," Hugh said. Entering the flats and up four flights of stairs, Hugh banged on a door and waited. The door opened slowly to reveal a brunette girl about 5ft 4inches, slim build wearing a blue nightie. She smiled and invited us in. I tried not to stare as she was attractive and diverted my eyes around the room, where I saw a guy sitting on the couch, which I presumed was her boyfriend.

This is Carla Malc Hugh said, as he steered me towards her. "Nice to meet you, Carla," "Ooh, you're a polite one." She said, "let's talk in this room" as she pulled on my arm...... "What, wait, wait, hold on, isn't that your boyfriend," I said? "Oh no, that's just my mate, Hugh wants to talk to him in private." "Hugh, let us know when you are finished," she said. Carla pulled on my wrist, leading me to a room where she turned the lights on and shut the door. The room had a double bed and a small bedside table with a lamp, blue curtains and smelling of scented candles. "Relax, sit down," Carla said, as I sat with her next to me. Looking up at me, she was smiling and trying to make eye contact. I was completely thrown out by this and felt nervous like I was in danger, but how could Carla be a danger to me, she didn't look violent.

Carla asked me if I liked her as she put her hand on my thigh, which ended up in a surprising position. Gobsmacked and before I could respond, Carla stood up in front of me and took off her nightie to reveal her naked breasts. Pushing on my chest, so I lay flat on the bed, she jumped on top of me.

The details of the next 30 minutes are not included, but it's important to mention that at some point, Carla left the room and come back with a pipe with a large white rock in the centre of the ash. How Carla got me to smoke this, again, is not needed, but she obviously knew what she was doing, and I'm sure I wasn't the first guy she had control of in this way. I was in triple ecstasy and could have quite happily died there and then. I knew the pipe-smoking was off the scale incredible, but I had no idea how it changed when under the spell of alluring sexy women.

After some time, maybe an hour, we returned to the front room where Hugh and the other guy smiled and laughed. "Hey…. how are you doing shouted Hugh? "Great thanks," "How are you?" Were good man, here I have got this for you, as he reached out another pipe with the most gigantic rock I've ever seen. "Is that for me I said?" "Yep, all yours Malc." By now, I was really craving another hit and my eyes just expanded when I saw the size of that rock.

"Wow, cheers Hugh" Knowing that this must be very expensive and holding the pipe to my mouth I took the deepest inhalation I could until the rock had sizzled into nothing before my eyes, exhaling in a cloud which seemed to be never-ending. Seconds later, I was face down on the floor, panting for my life as the high smashed into my face like a swirling tsunami wave. Carla was hitting another rock and Hugh, and this guy was admiring her style.

After five minutes, I was able to get up and felt just incredible. From feeling like I was about to die to a feeling like an angel had taken away all my fear, pain, worry and stress, everything in human nature that feels shit was gone, and every type of good feeling one can have was timed by a thousand. This was turning out to be a fantastic night, and just then, Hugh asked me if I wanted to try something new? In my alcoholic drugged upstate, I agreed, and Hugh took control. I cannot explain my next actions, just that I was incredibly smashed on crack cocaine. The next thing I knew I was falling onto the couch with a feeling of bliss, then quickly a feeling of sleepiness.

I closed my eyes, and my arm dropped off the side of the couch, still with the belt attached.

I woke, to Hugh and this other lad in a state of panic, asking me if I was alright and talking close to my face as each one held me under my armpits. It took me a short while to understand what they were saying to me and what had happened. At first, it was like being blurred sighted with the sound turned down. I was inside my body but seemed to be inside a fishbowl, looking at the frantic faces.

It seems they had been walking me around the flat for fifteen minutes with my feet dragging on the floor unconscious, slapping my face hard to regain consciousness as I had overdosed.... on heroin.

Hugh looked in shock but relieved that I was conscious, and swiftly announced it was time for us to go, asking me if I could walk "I think so, I replied" Standing up took all my effort. It felt like I was on the waltzers on a fairground, the floor seemed to move, and I was too unsteady on my feet. Hugh put one arm under my armpit and led me to the door, where Carla and this lad stood. Hugh past Carla some money as we exited. Carla gave me a kiss on the cheek saying, "bye babe." I guess Hugh was paying Carla for earlier and on reflection, it would appear the whole night was a setup, not that I realized at that time.

Hugh let go of me as we approached the car, and I nearly fell on the grass as I was still very much under the influence of what they had given me. I remember getting into the car and resting my face on the cold glass passenger window, vaguely able to see as we made our way back home. I was doing all I could not be sick, and the water was building in my mouth always. My mind and body appeared to be in full submission to death, the closest I have been to this would be counting backwards from ten in an operating theatre, just numb, silent, and thoughtless.

I awoke to Hugh, shouting my name, and with a few minutes of explanation, I understood he was saying we were home. "okay, okay, I will see you later then Hugh," as I struggled to get out of the car and stand up. I remember getting to my door was a great effort, wishing the pain and the measure of walking would stop as I entered the house and fell on the couch. It was daylight now, perhaps 5 am.

There would be no fishing competition for me that day or the next, as I got my wife to phone in sick for me as I lay in bed, slipping into semi unconsciousness over three days. It was Tuesday when I finally got out of bed, and obviously, I felt like shit, but I was alive by some miracle.

It took me three more days to become myself again, six days after that night. I was not myself at work, feeling lost inside, nervous, lonely, disappointed in myself, thinking I was a failure in life. Still, my most prominent thought was that I was a charlatan, a hypocrite no better than the people I arrest. I had somehow lost my identity and what I stood for. How quickly my life had changed due to my poor choices.

At that point, in my mind, I was sure I would shortly make a decision that would result in my life-ending, however, my past behaviour would suggest I was looking for death in a subconscious way.

Feeling really agitated with an incredible thirst for just one more crack pipe, in my mind, I couldn't think about anything else, anxiety overwhelmed me, a restlessness had consumed my biological needs.

I planned in my mind when I could go out with Hugh again, but never, was I going to make the mistake of using heroin again, at least that's what I told myself.

It was a Friday night when I decided I need to see my mate Jim, no alcohol for me this night as I drove to Jim's house and was met by a warm welcome as usual. Although his dad was a bit scary being five foot nothing of pure ripped muscle and a master in Bushido. Jim's parents were lovely. Yeh, you didn't want to piss his dad off for sure!

I went up to Jim's room, and we started talking about how things were and life at which point Jim said, "What the hell's going on with you, Malc?" I could tell he was disappointed in me, and he viciously suggested I sort my f****g life out, which was a fair statement, one only said by a best friend.

"Yes, I replied, your absolutely right Jim, I will, after just one or two more trips out then I'm done with all that."

"Your addicted," he said, "you're now a crack head!" "Your life will spiral out of control, you're going to lose everything, and then you will either end up in prison or dead." Fact! "This is not you, Malc!"

I didn't have much to come back on what Jim Said, he was always a wise, intelligent, level-headed guy, but what could I say? He was right. I usually left Jim's feeling great, but not this time, now I hated myself even more.

Returning home and not going to the pub, I had an unusual experience of sitting with my family, watching TV, and communicating with my wife. She obviously knew there was something seriously wrong with me that I wouldn't talk about. She knew of my war against our towns and cities' criminals, but I could tell by how she looked at me that she was aware that I was becoming more lost as the day's past. That night I remember going to bed before my children as I felt my presence made them all feel uncomfortable; perhaps it was because they didn't know who this stranger was sitting on the couch. I realized then; I had lost them, and they would be better off without me.

The following morning, I woke early, showered, swallowed down my handful of anabolic's and headed off to the gym with my protein shake.

Time passed quickly, and it was eight-thirty before I knew it, leaving the gym feeling much better and pumped looking strong. After a quick second shower and into my uniform, I was now back through my department store's doors. I didn't have long left here before my transfer, and I was keen to go out on a bang, monitoring the radio for signs of my real-life antagonist, which I had presumed he had been jailed as I hadn't seen him for ages since my attack. I wasn't sure if he had moved areas or even if he was dead.

Early afternoon I received a call from Mike One asking for my help. He was on the internal cameras, and an IC3 male was loitering around by the leather jacket rack. As I entered and placed myself in a position where I had a clear view, I called into CCTV with his description. IC3 male six foot four inches, sizeable stocky build, shaven head, brown scruffy leather jacket, and blue jeans. He was picking up different leather jackets and looking at the hangers and inside the seams. He was looking for security tags.

I called town centre CCTV to put the cameras on the front doors and observed in clear view this male now starting to pile jackets off the hangers over his right arm. I couldn't believe my eyes when this male had collected nine jackets piled over one arm. Calling on my radio for all guards to assist and any town centre police available, I observed this male walking toward the front doors. "All Call Signs Stand by, stand by, he's about to exit with non-payment." "Three, two, one. Wait, Wait, Stand down, all call signs stand down, he's dropped the lot at the front door," turning and sticking his fingers up to me as he walked casually out the door, past the guards and store detectives that were all ready to pounce. Smiling and laughing, he walked back up to the town square. "Well, that was a waste of manpower" I signaled to all call signs, apologizing, and thanking them for their help. Mike One couldn't believe it, at least thirty minutes had past homing in every camera on this male. After speaking with Mike One and agreeing to go to my loading bay for a cigarette, we walked towards the front of his store where we heard a shout, "Hey, you two," We turned around, and an angry-looking male in a smart suit was stomping rapidly towards us, it was Mike one's store manager. "They've taken all the alcohol from the shelf at the back of the store. All of it, three trolleys full. They were seen pushing the trolleys up a ramp into the end of a transit van."

"They're gone now." "And so is all the stock!" Racing to the back, we couldn't believe it, the shells where the whiskey, vodka, and gin had been displayed were now empty, running outside into the back-car park, there was no one to be seen. "Bloody hell, we've been had," I said to Mike One. The customer that had seen this had now left the store, and no one had taken her details. All the cameras were on the front doors, and now Mike One would have to sit through the tapes before giving any information to the police and CCTV. What a nightmare! I thought that was a massive bulk theft.

The afternoon was drawing to a close when I was called to assist Toby from the CCTV room as he was in pursuit of a female he had observed committing a theft while he was on his break in the town. The chase seemed to go on forever; this girl was fast and was already almost out of the cities viewing capabilities for CCTV coverage. Toby and I chased this criminal over fences through hedges, roads, and parks until we finally stopped her escape. Toby went in for the arrest first, and this girl who was all of five foot three inches, slim build with long dark hair kicked off royally. She must have been only eighteen, but she was like a feral cat. It took both of us to detain her safely while spitting at us and kicking us at every chance taken. As the police entered the park while she was face down on the grass with her arms in a lock, I couldn't help but think, women, can be the most aggressive to detain even when they are only eighteen. Maybe it's because we are men and don't want to hurt them, but my goodness she was a handful.

It was dark now, Toby thanked me for the assistance, and I headed back to the store to close. I felt the need for a pint and decided to go straight to the pub without changing my uniform. Around six-thirty in the evening, I pushed through the doors entering the bar being welcomed by five hating faces of the local dickheads. "Oh, fuck off," I thought as I turned my back to them and ordered my beer. Controlling my inner urge to let rip on these bullies was always a tasking dilemma. My inner rage just wanted to smash the f**k out of them, unforgivingly, allowing them to see the true nature that had reawakened within me, but always that voice of trying to be on the right side of the law would frustratingly prevent me. That voice really pissed me off sometimes.

Revenge

Friday was upon me, and I started to feel normal again, but I was still fighting that craving for more crack, struggling to take my mind off it to think and function correctly. Loaded up on more steroids, coffee, nicotine, and red bull, I was particularly alert and up for some action at work that day, eager to respond to anyone needing help and then came in the call of all calls.

"Delta Two from Mike One, Whiskey Kilo is exiting my store with confirmed items selected and concealed, with observed exit with non-payment in clear view."

That was him, that f***g b****d that assaulted me. My blood boiled instantly; my face contorted into a raged psychotic look. My panic was if someone else detained him, taking away this one chance, I had waited so long. At that single moment, with everything that was going through my mind, I was the most dangerous, unstable individual in the whole town with only one goal, him, Whiskey Kilo.

I started to calmly walk through the store towards the nearest exit, in a fake demeanour, so no one could see how furious, raged, and vengeful I felt. Out the side exit calling CCTV, "Charley one to Delta Two, do you have eyes on Whiskey Kilo?" "Yes, Charley One, He is just entering the town centre." "Thank you Delta Two, can you show me responding?" "Delta Two to Charley One, yes, yes, I've got the cameras on him now."

I was breaking into a run, cunningly planning that I needed to hold back until I could detain him in a zone off camera. It was excruciating, as all I wanted to do was rip his f****g throat out there and then in front of hundreds of shoppers. My decision was final. My life was over; I hated everything about my life and myself. Going to prison would be the best thing for me. I smiled the biggest smile as my mind permitted me to f**k him up bad. It all made sense with a feeling of euphoria. It was my destiny; this was the answer to all my pain. Entering the town centre calling Delta Two "Charley One to Delta Two, where is he now? Over." "Charley One, he just entering the alleyway to go towards the graveyard, black jacket, blue jeans, white trainers." "Got that Delta Two."

My eyes scanned the shoppers like a tiger viewing wilder beasts, and then, There! I spotted him, going out of view into the alleyway. Entering a full sprint, I was behind him within five seconds, thirty feet from his back. I slowed down as I could see people walking towards him, entering the town. I couldn't do it in full view of children and parents, wait, wait, slowly making my move, my heart was pounding. Wait, wait, patience, let them pass, approaching a grassed area, wait, wait, moving in......my breath was panting full of excruciating feelings of nervousness and anger. Becoming out of breath, then that split second where I was to make that final decision, once past there would be no turning back. "Fuck him!" he's going down! Accelerating up to a sprint for the remaining ten feet, anger rising by the second to a point where I was bursting with fury making contact with him at full strength, powered with a war cry from the deepest parts of my soul. Grabbing him with maximum speed while almost passing him. I was twisting my body in a circular motion in front of him, as I launched him into full karate throw. Entirely over my body upside down in the air, landing him crashing hard onto the grass, with his back down, facing my crazed psychotic roar as I screamed the most profound evil growl from my sickest Scottish ancestral pits.

Pulling him off the ground, twisting his jacket in both my hands as I moved his face touching his nose with mine, I continued to let out my fury screaming in his face terrifying his spirit.

His reaction to being surprised, thrown, and dropped with such horror and aggression was shocking. Immediately, trying to curl up into a ball, crying profusely, like a scared, defenceless little child. With howls and screams that I've only heard from sheer terror, sheltering his face with his arm as he looked upon my raged face. Shaking with fear, begging me to stop, "please, please don't."

I was instantly stunned by his reaction, and it stopped me in my tracks. I could not be this person that causes such horror attacks as he did with me. He was pathetic, a bully with his true colour showing, quivering on the floor, crying, howling, begging me to stop.

In that split second, I could see what had happened. I had become the aggressor, and he had become the victim.

I could not hurt him as now I pitied him. There may have been a hundred wrong things in my life, but I would never hurt an innocent person with violence. Yes, he deserved to get f****d up for the sickening attack on myself and so many others, but if I did, I would be as bad as he was, and the simple truth was, I couldn't, my very essence and nature couldn't inflict harm. I was born with an innate impulse to protect, not hurt. "F**k," I was being torn one way by good and pulled in the opposite direction with evil.

Telling him to turn over face down with his hands behind his back and stay still, I called Delta Two for a police response to my location, which was confirmed ETA in five minutes as the patrol car was close. He started to talk to me, saying he was sorry for stealing the jumpers from Mike One, to which I told him to shut his f****g mouth.

He was still the b****d that assaulted me; I was a happily married father who was innocent of any wrongdoing until this despicable piece of shit attacked me. The last thing I was going to do was talk to him.

"Stay f****g there and don't f****g move," I shouted; the police will be here in a minute".

Feeling a bit relieved to see a police car pull up, two officers approached us, and quickly put him in cuffs, leading him away with his head hanging down in shame and defeat. That view there, is the real price of crime.

Walking back to my store and quickly making my way to the café for a takeaway coffee on route to the loading bay for a cigarette. Sitting down with my first deep drag, I reflected for one moment: I got the b****d; at last, I had him. Also, I didn't assault him or snap his f****g neck. Okay, I scared the shit out of him and took him down a bit hard, which was still wrong, but considering what he did to me, I think he got off very lightly.

That night at home, I was elated to tell my wife that I had nailed someone I had been looking for a long time. I was so pleased, and I would celebrate in the pub later for sure.

Already into my fourth pint by 7 pm, I was well on my way to getting drunk, and as it was Friday night, the bar was becoming busy. Sending a text to Hugh that I was in the pub and we needed to celebrate, he responded to say he would be up in thirty minutes.

I wanted to go out, I enjoyed that hit, I craved that hit, but tonight I thirst to inhale a record size rock ever. I had to have it; every cell screamed for that first magical, euphoric hit. Sinking another well-deserved three pints just as Hugh turned up, it was no time before we were hurtling back to Telford to score another fat rock of crack. Oh, I was so excited and told Hugh about my day and how I had finally nailed the b****d that assaulted me. Hugh was laughing and giggling, "f****g hell." he said, "you should've kicked his f*****g teeth down his throat and stamped on his head. Jesus."

I thought that's ruthless thinking, but I understood his notion that I should have put great pain on him. For months I had believed I would when I got my hands on him, training, running, all in preparation for that one moment, and then I couldn't do it; it just wasn't me.

I was wrestling with my head's thoughts, but deep down in my gut, I knew I did the right thing. It almost seemed I was a disappointment to Hugh, which kind of killed my joy.

It wasn't long before we settled into a discrete country location, after another dodgy transaction in some dark, secluded car park. It was the most significant chunk of crack I had ever seen, the size of a one penny piece. It was massive, and the cost was ridiculous, but the need, carvings, and celebration, outweighed common sense or any token of morality or sensibility; we were addicts now. Nothing meant as much as a large rock, which had now become all I ever really thought about, that euphoric hit.

"My turn first, I said to Hugh," cut me off a f**k off first hit." He smiled and quickly broke off a quatre of the rock. "No way am I taking all that Hugh, cut that in half I said," "No, you'll be in heaven, it will be a great hit, you are celebrating go for it."

Blimey, I had never come close to taking the size of crack like this, exciting and nervous at the same time. I raised the red bull pipe to my mouth and lite the process pea-size glistening chunk of pure bliss. It sparked, crackled, and hissed as it slowly began to melt away into a pure vapour demonic kiss. Struggling to hold in the humongous inhalation it took to do the hit in one, I slowly exhaled the entire rock of smoke from my lungs, and then, here it comes, that first, crystal pure hit of the first pipe of the night.

It blew my head off, and the escalating rise just kept going higher and higher, panting like I was going to give birth, trying everything in my power to ride out the initial peak, eyes bulging, gripping the car seat tight. Hugh was laughing like fuck to my reaction. I couldn't speak, concentrating, waiting for the roller coaster to reach the top of the ride so that I could plateau. At this point, the hit turns from being uncomfortable to entirely out of this world euphoric, and here it comes. Slowly at first, then increasingly, taking me to a place of insane pleasure, like one hundred orgasms at once that last continuously none stop for twenty to thirty minutes. That is the best way I can describe it. I was floating in a sea of pleasure, one thousand times greater than I had ever experienced in my life, what an insane hit.

Hugh went large too and was panting in the seat next to me, which allowed me to laugh at him now, which was funny for me, but not for him. After he had overcome the initial hit, we both just mellowed out into a cauldron of giggles, laughter, and euphoric waves of pleasure, pulsing through our bodies from the tips of our fingers to the toes on our feet. It was the best feeling ever.

Several pipes later, it was all gone, and we were just a mess, talking shit, laughing at stupid shit, trying to speak but talking like a very drunk asshole, forgetting what we were trying to say halfway through the conversation, just a mess.We talked for a couple of hours later and decided we would look for more in Wolverhampton, where Hugh knew a few guys and off we went. It was now 1 am.

Arriving at a dodgy council estate in Wolverhampton, Hugh knocked on a door, and shortly later, two girls jumped into the car with us so that they could show Hugh directions to a house he wanted to go. Their names were Karen and Sophie. Karen was a thin girl, about thirty, lots of wrinkles on her face with thin dyed blond hair. She appeared to jump around in the seat, sniffing and twitching. A polite girl as she kissed me on the cheek from the back seat and said, "Hey, Malc." Sophie was a younger girl about twenty-one, didn't speak much, but smiled and looked out the car window, staring into the night. The car navigated the concrete jungle of depravity as we hurtled towards our destination, it was about two o'clock in the morning now.

We were arriving at a dark and sinister location that resembled a tower block where we all jumped out of the car and entered the dimly lit stairway. Graffiti on the lifts and walls, and a strong smell of piss, we started to climb to the fourth floor. Hugh was knocking a secret knock on a door, where we were all welcomed inside.

The flat guy called Brian; was a white male, six-foot-tall, medium build with short blonde hair with a prison hard life look. "Come in guys and have a seat," he welcomed us. I sat down on this, not so excellent looking couch, and Sophie sat next to me while Karen, Hugh, and Brian went into the kitchen. "You alright, Sophie?" I asked, "Not bad, Malc," "bit tired and knackered," she replied. "What are you doing hanging around with Hugh?" she asked. "Oh, I know him from my village and, we became mates," I replied. "You don't look the type to be playing this game Malc; you've got kind eyes," She said. Before I could respond to Sophies' kind words, Hugh came into the room and said, "Alright guys, let's go." We all said goodbye to Brian, down the stairs, and back into the car, where we headed back to Wolverhampton, but this time, Karen asked if she could sit in the front with Hugh, and Sophie with me in the back which was fine.

Karen was telling Hugh a story about her kids going into care and how she was adamant about getting them back, becoming upset often. I asked Sophie how life was for her, "things all good?" "Yeh not great, to be honest, I have to work every day." "Oh, what do you do?" I asked, as she looked at me and smiled, "Your cute honey." Not replying, I guess it was an answer saying if you must ask you don't need to know.

Sophie was resting her head on my shoulder with her arm across my waist, and she half lay down on the back seat being so tired. Ten minutes into the drive, as we picked up speed on the dual carriageway, Sophie whispered in my ear "Hey Malc, you're a nice smart lad and you smell real nice, for twenty quid if you like I will do something for you?" as she lowered her head into my lap. "No, no, I whispered, thanks, but no." "It's okay; I'm fine." "You're different from the rest, Malc. I like you," She replied and smiled, placing her head on my lap to try to sleep. After twenty minutes, we were back at the girl's house, where Hugh and Karen got out and exchanged some money and stuff. Sophie, putting her hand on my shoulder, leaning forward, and giving me an arousing sexy slow kiss, said, "Have a good life, Malc," smiling as she got out of the car. I liked Sophie; she was lovely.

Soon we found ourselves parked up in some dark country lane where we got on with our usual business of large rocks, laughter, and talking shit. But something was different deep down inside, and I couldn't describe it. We watched the sun come up as we sat, once again on the devils thrown caressed by a hundred orgasms and our euphoric delusions until Hugh turned the key, and a short time later, we were minutes away from home. Pulling up and thanking Hugh, I said I would see him later as he smiled and drove off as I unusually stopped on my path and watched Hugh drive out of view. It was seven in the morning now, so I decided to shower and go straight to work although something felt strange.

Airborne Police Chase

Having breakfast in the café before starting, I felt peculiar, not sick, but empowered with a form of troubled clarity you could say, almost like being in deep contemplation. However, I didn't stay that way much into the morning, when an unusual call sign came on to the radio asking for emergency assistance at Papa 3.

"Charley One to Papa three, where is your location?" I responded, once she replied, I understood where she was, which was a comfortable mile and a half away from my location. I paused for a moment, thinking I could make it in about nine or ten minutes. "Papa three to Charley one, are you receiving over." "Yes, Yes, go ahead Papa three," "Charley one he's filling his jacket with everything, I'm on my own here, can you please help. "On route now, Papa three," I responded. My decision was made, a girl needed my help. I was into a full run within seconds, dodging members of the public as I made my way to the other side of the town, nearly everyone was looking at me. I was almost at a maximum sprint as I propelled towards the roundabout, over the metal railings, over three lanes of traffic, onto the roundabout, running through it to navigate the three roads once more. Entering the outskirts of the town and into an industrial estate, I still had half a mile to go, as I was starting to slow slightly, but still maintained a good pace, a few minutes later I could see the store as I called Papa three. "Approaching your location now Papa three, where is this male now." "Charley, one from Papa three, he's just leaving now, standing outside the door six-foot, green jacket brown short hair, over." He was standing in clear view when he looked up and saw me running towards him. Jumping over a wall and into the car park that led to the front doors, he now knew I was coming for him, and he bolted. My god, he can run, as I increased my pace as we both were now in the central reservation running towards ongoing traffic. Crossing the two lanes and into a subway, with three ways to go, I figured he was going for a estate and made the right subway turn, getting back on his heals within a few moments. Up to three flights of concrete steps, and we were back heading out of town, passing Esporta fitness centre. CCTV called with a broken message that they are going to lose me any minute as we were running out of radius for the radios to work, and we had passed the last camera on the outskirts of the town.

I was not bothered about this, nor did I reply, to me he was a target, an enemy, and I was not going to give up the chase as he swung into a lane that crossed into a disused railway track set deep down an embankment. It was like a path dug into the ground, forty feet below the surface. I continued closing in on him as he fell down another decline into a forest area. Still panicked struck that I was still coming after him, up into a large open field, I took chase ten meters behind him out of the lot at the other end, and onto an adjacent road. We were now approaching an area that didn't come under the legislations our city. The chase had covered four miles by now, and I figured it was time this lad went down. I could hear a police helicopter above my head, which I was astonished but grateful thinking "go on boys," I shouted, sirens echoed all around me as three police cars closed in. Seeing this, the lad just stopped dead and stood still, giving himself up whilst I secured him in an arm lock, allowing him to stand as I felt he was not a danger. He had ditched all the stock he had stolen, but it didn't matter as we had internal CCTV footage and eyewitness accounts of the theft.

The police took his sorry arse off to the station, and I lit up a cigarette and started my very long walk back to the town, as the three police cars slowly passed, one shouting out his window, "excellent job Malc," which I thought was nice, but a lift would have been better!

Back in my store Toby from CCTV came to see me, to say congratulations for catching such an energetic criminal over such a distance. He said several police officers were watching in the CCTV room, and on monitors in the police station as well as airborne cameras zoomed in. Many people were in admiration of your firm will, perseverance, and fitness. "Arrr, that's nice, thanks, but it's not necessary" I thanked Toby.

"It's was nice to be recognized, but I didn't need any of that stuff," I said to him as we walked to the loading bay for a cigarette. "Some you win and some you lose, and today you won Malc," Toby said.

Feeling happy at the end of my shift around 18.30, I walked towards my car park past Iceland into the back streets off camera. A route I have taken a hundred times.

Suddenly, I was jumped on by three well known criminals, two who were brothers. They went into full attack, punching and kicking me. I jumped back into a karate stance as one lad flew at me with a wide swinging punch, raising my left arm high and blocking it, grabbing hold of his arm, I connected with an elbow which stunned him. One lad went behind me, and he received a back kick to his chest just as I got punched in the face. I moved out into the middle of the road to get some distance from them and another came running at me, connecting with a front kick to his chest. Another punch to the back of my head sent me dizzy as another lad flew in with a kick to my back. I was in trouble here and strictly needed to end this. Going on the attack jumping forward with a punch to the side of one lads head, he hit the floor. Receiving another punch, then a kick from the remaining two, I had little choice. I was exhausted and soon I would be overpowered. A striking kung fu chop to the right side of his collar bone sent him collapsed unconscious to the floor as the final guy looked at his mate and screamed in rage with both hands going for my neck. Dropping down to his knee height in a crouching stance and upper cutting his private parts dropped him like a stone.

One lad still unconscious, one lad buckled up in pain with his testicles in his mouth and the other lad getting up and trying to run away. F**k me! I thought, dam I was in pain again and still feeling dizzy as I staggered towards the covered runway past Iceland leading to Sierra Ones location which was the nearest store open till 10pm.

I thanked Sierra One after we had a cigarette and a coffee outside his loading bay, as he called it in to CCTV and a short time after, I headed off to my car escorted by Sierra One. Within thirty minutes, I was home and told my wife I had been attacked but managed to get them off me. She suggested I should think about leaving this job as it was going to kill me one day. I agreed.

I walked into the bedroom and once again looked at my body in the mirror, which to be honest I didn't care about how bad I looked, I just wanted a hug from someone, that was all, yes I looked awful, but I was alive. I got into bed and stayed there for three days, getting up occasionally for a cigarette, fluid and tiny amounts of food then going straight back to bed, in that time I lost a stone in weight as my body attempted to heal itself.

Hugh had knocked on my door a couple of times whilst I was in bed, insisting on talking to me, but my wife wouldn't let him in. She didn't like him as she thought he was responsible for my downturn, but really it was I who had made the choices. Whilst I was in bed in and out of sleep, I would have nightmares of being set on fire and being stamped on. It was a dark place to be in as I recall when my wife went to work, I would often cry into my pillow so much that I would end up with a headache. I remember waking feeling relieved to be safe in bed and not burning alive. This seemed to be the end of the road for me. My time as a guard was over, and I called my security company to tell them. They told me my area manager Ian would be in contact with me, and one day later, there was a knock on my door.

Ian was a stocky tall six-foot-four male with blonde hair and ex para corporal; he suggested my time was up in this town and that he will move me instantly to the top store in Birmingham as supervising guard. He told me there were too many criminals out for my blood, and it clearly was not safe for me anymore, the bounty on my head was too high and that I had put away too many of them. I agreed with him but was still reluctant. Ian said, "I have told our millionaire boss of your record and what had happened to you."

"He has sent me to see you with a blank cheque as he wants to compensate you for your injuries and trauma." Ian got out this cheque and a pen. Looking at me sternly, he said, "so how much will it cost Malcolm to keep you?"

I was obviously shocked and didn't want to be an asshole, so I paused and said: "A good weeks pay to cover me whilst I have been off, and some injury compensation would be acceptable." We came to a generous mutual agreement, and after finishing his coffee and arranging for a new uniform to be sent to me, Ian shook my hand and left. I felt valued and needed by someone, which was nice.

Bulk Snatch

Ten days had passed since being attacked, and I was feeling nervous about stepping back into my role as a guard, but bills needed paying, and I was hoping my next store would be safer with other guards to support me, including plainclothes store detectives.

The train journey through Wolverhampton into Birmingham New street was packed with people hurrying to their place of work and colleges. Looking at some of them, I often thought about how oblivious they appeared to be in their own bubble.

Finding my new store was easy as it was one of the leading stores in the city, entering through the second floor, which opened into the high street and instantly seeing a guard who gave me the directions to the security room. I made my way through the extravagant shop layout, up two flights of escalators locating the door and being welcomed in. Tanya was the CCTV operator and was excited to meet me. "I've heard great things about you, Malcolm." "I am keen to stabilize the store's security team." Tanya was five foot five, white female, slim build with long dark hair and blue eyes, she was in her early thirties and was clearly experienced as she gave me a rundown of the situation. Tanya showed me three books of criminal's photos that were known to the store and had been highlighted in the city centre crime watch program. Most of them looked like they were straight out of prison, and I started to think these criminals might be a whole new level.

After setting me up with my radio and briefing, Tanya locked up the office while she escorted me to the basement, where there were two cells for detained individuals. "Blimey, I said, they are the real deal, metal doors with a kind of padding wall with a fixed pine bench on the back wall." Tanya handed me a key and said, "you'll be wanting this." "You have five guards on at any one time with two store detectives, so your team is seven." "We have the food hall on the basement floor and three other floors that also lead to a shopping centre." "On average, we manage to detain around eight a day."

That first day we detained six individuals for shoplifting and credit card fraud, all of them straight forward with a little breathless sprinting but all without world war three erupting.

The camera system was brilliant, and Tanya was fantastic too, she really looked out for the guard's safety, which was nice to see.

The store detectives who basically walked around like they were shopping, with a see-through earpiece didn't like to be seen detaining people as it blew their cover, so they would act as a witness to selection, concealment, and exit without payment.

The guards would be positioned on every floor with two guards and a store detective on the first-floor monitoring people coming in and out of the high street. The first week we racked up thirty-five detained individuals, where I would be in charge of interviewing them, retrieving the stolen stock, taking their picture and banning them from the store, and then entering them onto the crime watch program.

Not all were arrested by the police, as we had to calculate the severity of the crime, in balance with the current city crime level.

Taking officers of the ground in the city would reduce the response available to severe incidents, and as such, myself and Tanya would decide if the police were called. Out of the thirty-five detained, only twelve were arrested and taken off in the bracelets of shame.

While in the detaining room, many individuals would volunteer their stories, and it was a shocking and eye-opening encounter.

Sarah, a white female, aged just nineteen, was detained for stealing jewellery from the vogue section, she was five foot two, medium build with short ginger hair. Sarah had been sleeping on the streets ever since she was seventeen after her stepdad raped her and then beat her unconscious. Telling her that he would kill her mom if Sarah ever told anyone, so Sarah ran away. Having no address, she could not claim any benefits, had no family support, and thus decided to hide in toilets on the train from London to Birmingham.

Since the two years sleeping rough with the occasional refuge centre stay, she had been attacked ten times, held down and molested, had beer cans thrown at her, and had her remaining belongings stolen while she slept. She had been drugged several times, become addicted to heroin in a cry to forget, and had woken up in an alleyway with her underwear around her ankles three times.

She was shoplifting for money to buy heroin. Her story broke my heart, and I was fighting back the tears, listening to her. I couldn't believe how flippant she was about everything that had happened to her like it was no big deal, but her eyes told me she was telling the truth. I had no words after hearing her story.

Tom or Tommie, he liked to be called, was jailed for theft at eighteen after his third offence. He was five foot eight inches, slim build, freckles, and a Manchester accent, he was now twenty-three. He told me that he used to steal to buy food as his mom was a single parent and a heroin addict. He often missed school as a teenager and, as such, didn't do too well in his exams and ended up leaving school with no qualifications. His mom would cry so much when she ran out of her fix, that this would also spur him to go out on the rob as he put it. In jail, he was assaulted many times and experienced sexual abuse in his first sentence of six months. Hearing his story was bad enough but listening to the silent scream under his voice was unbearable.

Amanda was a thirty-five-year-old woman, five foot ten, slim build with curly dark hair, and glasses. She was from a well-known area outside Birmingham. She was detained for stealing vodka from the food hall. She told me that she had her three children taken into care after she got hooked on crack cocaine. It all started with the children missing school, and then social services stepped in.

With anonymous calls to the police for child safeguarding issues, the children got removed under a child protection order. Spiraling into her own darkness from the pain of losing her children, she started smoking more crack, and with one thing after another, she found herself prostituting on the back streets of Birmingham and along the canal paths. Amanda had been put into hospital five times, ran over, raped at knifepoint, and controlled by a pimp. She wanted me to call the police to have her arrested, in the hope she would be charged and locked up, hoping for a sentence inside the prison.

I just wanted to hug her, but I knew I couldn't. These are only three stories in one week, and the reality of how cruel life could be for so many people out there was rapidly dawning on me.

The commute each day was discomforting as I would leave home at seven in the morning and return home at nine or ten o'clock at night after completing my twelve-hour daily shift. I hadn't been to the pub in my village all week, returning straight home as the twelve hours and travelling were more demanding than my last location, and I was trying to make a good impression.

While at work, I would constantly monitor the radio from other store guards. It was clear that shoplifting was a prolific problem in this city centre, perhaps merely because of the tens of thousands of shoppers, meaning a higher ratio of thieves and, therefore, a higher risk to the guard. However, with more stories being volunteered, the more I wished I could help them. They were all someone's sons and daughters who have either made poor choices in their life or have found themselves in an impossible situation where living on the streets was a safer option. Being someone who wants to help others, this was so difficult to listen to and worse as I felt powerless to help.

I was in my third week, and it was a Saturday when I was standing in the front of the store on the high street level opposite the ladies' designer clothing section, which was always a popular hit for shoplifting.

There were two double doors to my left leading into the street and two double doors on my right. Tanya in the CCTV room radioed me to say two suspicious males just came into the left double door area and dipped behind the clothing rails. I was right there in that position, and I could see the two males. One of them holding a large bin bag and the other, taking off a pile of hangers with the cloths attached and rolling them around his arm, quickly placing them into the bin bag.

Instantly I ran to the right double doors calling Tanya on my radio that there was a bulk selection in progress in the ladies' designer area. I was going outside to stop them both as they exited.

Running to the front of the doors they would be coming out of leading to the six steps, I knew they would go right and not run into a busy city centre where there were hundreds of cameras. I waited around the corner of the department store, peeping around the corner to make sure they were coming my way, and sure enough, seconds later, out they flew running down the stairs with two bin liners full of stock.

They accelerated around the corner at such a pace and spread apart. I was only able to close line one male to the pavement sending the bin liner of clothes flying into the side street.

Turning and taking chase accelerating to a sprint at once, I was on the second man's heels within ten seconds, where he had spotted me as he ran looking over his shoulder. As I got closer entering the bus station, he dumped the bag to diffuse my chase, but I sprinted past the stock and went over the metal railings with him, both of us smashing into the hard Perspex frame of a bus shelter.

Jumping up and back to a sprint, this lad was halfway across the bus station before I recovered from almost smashing my head open. I then considered it would be better to go back and retrieve the stock, radioing his description and location to the city centre CCTV to try to follow and pick up. Recovering the stock, heading back to my store, another guard had come out and retrieved the goods from the road, but the male had escaped unseen.

Tanya inspected the stock in the holding room and valued the total amount they would have got away with. Eight hundred and ninety pounds in total. All of which took place in less than two minutes. It was a good stop, and I felt good having a well-deserved coffee and cigarette after that one but reflecting, how professional and quick these guys were, and I wondered how many more like them would I encounter.

Returning home that day, I really fancied a beer but didn't want to meet Hugh, so I chose to buy some cans and go straight home. I had stopped taking my steroids as I had no time now to go to the gym. I didn't have much motivation or energy to do so. It had also been nearly three weeks since I had seen Hugh, and I was conscious of my high-profile position and work commitment. I didn't want to be doing anything that could screw that up. It seemed that my injuries, sleep, rest, and children's hugs had helped me over the thirst for nocturnal activities, and I was pleased this was the case.

Three days later, I detained a white male on the raw meat section's food aisle. Filling a bag with all the high-value steaks. He was six foot two, medium to stocky build with a black leather jacket and black jeans on. He came quietly and calmly to the first escalator on the first floor as we headed to the third-floor security office.

At the top of the first-floor escalator, he kicked off and went crazy. It was carnage. We both ended up tumbling down the escalator, mowing down customers as we fell on the hard, sharp metal moving steps. Falling down an escalator, especially a big one in a fight with a muscular guy, is a terrible day. I must have looked like Freddie Kruger had attacked me, I was shredded to bits by the steps' sharp teeth, and he was too. Landing at the bottom, but with the belt still running on the steps. We were just tumble dried over and over each other until someone finally hit the stop button on the escalator.

This guy was placed into the cells while we waited for the police.

Going straight to the A and E to get treatment, and shocked at how bad I looked stripped naked behind the cubicle. It was like being thrown off a motorcycle with a T-shirt on. I was in a great deal of pain, from lower legs to my head, front and back as I was covered in injuries more than ever before. The hospital advised me to go home and rest, and I hobbled slowly back to the taxi rank, which took me to the train station.

Again, at home, after my bath, I looked at the damage on my body. The bruising was terrible. Where every step hit, there was a mark, skin break, or blackening. My knees, elbows, sides, and thighs were the worst, with my face and hands showing cuts and grazes, I felt like a car had hit me, again.

Resting in bed with painkillers and plastered with Sudocreme, I took the next day off and stayed in bed to heal.

Jumping back on the train for another day, two hours after restarting work, I detained a Muslim woman in a full traditional gown, with her head and face covered. I was cautious not to touch her, as we had been told that if this could be avoided, just escort them to the holding room and wait for the police. She did not say anything, and at that point, I could give no description apart from she had blue eyes, which I thought a little odd. After saying we were going to call the police, retrieving the stolen perfume in her bag, she suddenly said, it is ok, you do not have to do that. Lifting her robe off her body to reveal she was, in fact, a man, not only a man but a well-known shoplifter who was banned from the city and Tanya quickly confirmed this.

I couldn't help but laugh at the ingenious way he had camouflaged his identity, adding to that, was the pink cream purse and the lady's shoes he was wearing. I thought, well, you couldn't make that up, could you? He had broken his conditions of the order upon him, so we had little option but to detain him until an officer could collect him.

Syringe Attack

It was a dark and miserable day as I stepped out of Birmingham train station, making my way to the store through the crowds of people hurrying about with their business as they knocked, ignored and glared at you on their way to work or University. There seemed to be something in the air today, a tension, like planets, had aligned and moon phase exactly right to cast over the city a sense of something coming.

No one I spoke to at work was in a good mood, everyone appeared tired and grumpy. The energy of people's aura seemed to be off-balance, and I just knew today was going to be a bad day. The store was busy but oddly quiet as people queued with a stern inpatient look in lines at the tills. The food hall was dead as people decided today was a day to stay at home rather than do a food shop.

I recall it was around midday when the call came through to my radio from the electronics department that a male was making off out of the store exiting into the shopping centre with a stolen plasma TV. Being on the first floor and the department calling was on the fourth floor, I decided my fastest route would be out into the high street taking a left and running up to the exit where this male would be coming out. I radioed the CCTV office to clarify his description.

I was not impressed to hear what I did. "IC3 male six-foot-six inches, large, stocky build, shaven head, tattoos on his face." Great I thought. How the hell am I going to stop him?

I just knew in my gut things were going to get awfully bad, very quickly as I panted with nervousness entering the shopping centre. Scanning around whilst hugging the side of a store, I waited and prepared for the male to come into view. He was not going to be hard to miss carrying a large plasma TV, and sure enough, his towering stature came into view. My God, this guy was huge! F**k he's going down I thought, I am having him, as I picked up pace heading directly in his path.

Coming to a halt directly in front of him with my right hand outstretched in a forcible stop sign he paused looking at me with disgust. "What the f**k do you want" he bellowed down at me. "Sir, there has been some discrepancy in the store where you have purchased your TV, and I am going to need you to follow me back to the store so we can clear it up."

"I don't f*****g think so," he said, as he tried to walk around me picking up pace with his long strides and bulky frame. "Oh f*****g hell I thought" here we go. Running up behind him, I grabbed his left arm with my right hand on his elbow, and my left hand on his left wrist, whilst he continued to hold the sizeable boxed TV. "What the f**k do you think you're doing" he yelped. "Sir, you're going to have to come back with me to sort this out as the store is reporting this TV has been stolen." "I paid for it on my credit card," he said. "Sir, do you have that receipt?" I asked. "Yes, as he put down the TV on the floor and started to look into his pockets. Stepping back slightly into a balanced karate foot stance expecting a surprise move by him, he did what I was so hoping he would not, kicking out a straight kick towards my chest. "F**k me," I thought as I stepped quickly to the side as his big foot narrowly missed launching me through the shop window. Grabbing him under the knee of his left leg still in the air with my right hand and raising it higher to throw him off balance and with my left leg, karate side kicking his right knee he fell like a tree being felled hard onto his arse. His big body frame crashing onto the polished floor of the shopping centre, whilst shoppers gasped as they made a large parameter as they shuffled past.

"Don't f****g think about it" I shouted down to him as he tried to get up. "I'm ex-forces mate, it's not f****g happening." Forcibly grabbing his jacket with both hands in a statement of confidence and authority, I pulled him into the position of kneeling and told him to stand up. As he did, I knew what I needed to do with this guy. Instantly I put his arm into a bent arm lock, then slid my right hand to his bent arm hand, placing him into a painful thumb lock. Raising his arm up to his back which anatomically forced his body to lean forward as I kept the motion flowing by spinning him around and frog-marching his arse back to the side entrance of the store through the shopping centre. Making sure to put enough pressure on his thumb to cause just enough pain and march him into quick pace still bent over with my left hand pushing down his neck, we entered the side entrance to my store taking him straight to the escalator on floor one towards the cells on the ground floor.

I was keen to get him into a cell as soon as possible as if he managed to get out of this lock, I had on him, it could end badly for me. "Don't add assault to a theft charge," I screamed at him as I put more pain on him, raising my thumb lock higher up his back as I reached for my keys to open the cell door. Placing him into the middle of the room before letting go and quickly getting out of there, slamming the cell door, and locking it. "F**k me" as I took a gasp, that arrest was insane, I cannot believe I got him without getting injured. I am not going back in there with him I thought, he can stay there till police officers come to collect him.

Laughing in relief to myself, I headed back out to the shopping centre where I met a guard who worked inside the centre. He handed me the TV and said, "Did you manage that one?" "Yes, I said, only just though." He laughed, turned, and walked back into the centre.

Taking the TV back to the section, I headed off for a takeaway coffee and a fag, being congratulated over the radio by Tanya in the

CCTV room. Blimey, I thought, drawing on my fag, like it was my last breath, I wonder what it would be like doing an office job? Surly I am meant for something else in life.

Within forty-five minutes, the CCTV footage and the male in the cells were collected by two officers, and I saw him being taken out the back of the store to a police van. "Thank God he's gone." I thought, as I made my way to the security room. "Malc, do you know who that guy was?" Tanya said, "No, Tanya, who was he?" "well-known Malc, he's a right headcase."

Sombre in my thoughts as I paused to answer, "Well, I'm glad I got to detain him without getting injured then." To be fair, I did think I was lucky, but technique, confidence and a military approach can go a long way in situations like that. I was pleased with the result.

Taking my lunch and enjoying it immensely as I tucked into my lasagne, salad and garlic bread I devoured half of it before being called into action again, this time in the food hall on the ground floor.

An elderly woman with a four-wheeled material shopping trolley was loading it full of shopping, rather than putting it into a basket or a store trolly. She was about eighty years old as I assessed whilst slowly moving in to speak to her. "Hello madam, are you alright there?" I said. "Oh, hello, young man, you look handsome in your uniform, don't you." she said. "Oh, thank you, do you know you should be putting your items into a basket rather than concealing them in your trolley?" "Oh, as she looked up with her hands and head shaking." Bless her I thought as I stepped back, she is no shoplifter, a mild illness is affecting her judgment here.

"What's your name my love?" I asked her, "Ooo my name is Clarence." "I tell you what Clarence, do you mind if I help you today with your shopping?" "Ooo that would be lovely she said."

Over the next thirty minutes, I organised her shopping into a trolley and walked with her supporting her arm as we went through her shopping list, sitting down occasionally to take a rest. Clarence was a lovely lady and just needed a little bit of help. I asked her how she was getting home, and she told me she came on the bus. After finding out where she lived and making sure she was clear and confident about her address, I paid for her taxi, and we walked to the collection point.

Clarence had taken up an hour of my time, but it was an absolute pleasure.

Now three o'clock and not long till I was finishing, but still patrolling the store looking for any suspicious behaviour when I spotted something. I could not believe what I had just seen, and I had no idea how to communicate this on the radio to Tanya. Behind the novelty shelves, there was an attractive woman five foot six, wearing a pretty floral dress, red heals on with short blonde hair. There was a man with her, both were in their thirties and what they were doing gobsmacked me instantly. This woman was hiding by the back shelf lifting her dress up to her waist to reveal her completely naked vagina area. This man was photographing her with a camera. "What the F**k", I thought. I turned my back to radio Tanya. "Tanya from Charley One, I've got an IC1 male and an IC1 female exposing themselves on the shop floor." "Received that Charley One, what location are they in and I will get the cameras on them." I turned back, and they were gone, scanning around quickly to see where they were, I just caught the back of them leaving the store through the front doors.

What do I do, I thought? Do I chase after them and detain them? I had not come across this scenario before, and it felt like a grey area. I decided I was not going to deal with this. What would I say to the city CCTV room if I reported this loud on the store watch radio for every shop security staff to hear? No, I am not going there with this I thought leaving them to go free on their way to whatever other location they had in mind for their pornographic photo shoot.

Five o'clock now, and it was starting to get dark outside, which is always a popular time to be hit by bulk snatchers and shoplifters. Patrolling on the second floor, I received a call to go to the furniture department where something was kicking off. Starting to run up the escalators, I approached the top floor and heard shouting.

A male and a female were at the desk shouting at the assistant. Moving in quickly, I approached the desk and instantly stood in front of this couple instructing them to calm down and stop screaming, which they did.

"What's going on here, I asked?" "They won't accept my credit card," said the girl. This couple was a young female in tracksuit bottoms, blonde waist-length greasy hair. She was wearing an Adidas white top about five foot four and the male was six foot skinny and skinny looking with a yellow tinge to his skin with a worn, tired look upon his face. Also, in his twenties, who was looking agitated.

There accent and language combined with their clothing and behaviour raised suspicion with me that their American Express card might be cloned or fake.

"Oh, I know what's happened here, Sir, Madam," I said, "We have been having a problem with our machines in-store, and we have seen this before." "Please come with me, and I will do a quick phone call from my office to verify the card, and we can resolve this straight away. You can then collect your goods with our apology.

"At last," the girl said, "some action." I raised out my arm in a royalty gesture for them to lead the way as we walked to the security room two floors down.

"Glad you came to help us mate, you're a sound bloke," said the male, "Oh it's okay, this kind of thing can happen," I said. I thought as we approached the office how blatantly oblivious this couple was about the reality of things as they sat down by a table with two chairs in the side room to our office. "Just let me make a quick phone call, and we will have you on your way in no time." "Cheers mate, you're a f****g star," said the lad.

Speaking to Tanya in the next room, keeping an eye on the door that was the exit, I asked Tanya to run a quick check on the card.

"Can I get you a cup of water?" I asked. "No, we're fair love, said the girl as they sat there confident with their position. Moments later, Tanya confirmed what I thought all along, the card had been stolen and had been cancelled.

Telling Tanya to call the police at once and to lock her door. I returned into the side room and said "I'm terribly sorry to inform you that the card has been reported stolen. So now you are both being detained for attempting to obtain goods by deception and the police have been called.

All I can say is what happened next was like a scene from an American wrestle mania. Chairs were being thrown, screaming, and shouting vulgar words at me, the table was launched at me, and these two just switched into psychos. Great another day at the office, I thought! As the female spat in my face, and the guy hit me with a plastic and metal chair hurting the side of my shoulder, I jumped into an urgent mode of dealing with this carnage.

The male launched forward at me with his arm swung back and I connected a sidekick to his hip which dropped him instantly, just then the female grabbed me around my neck in a chokehold from behind half jumping on my back. Trying to deal with the shock of my breathing being restricted, I jumped back, still with the girl holding on falling backwards onto the floor. Crushing her in doing so.

She let go of my throat just as the guy kicked me in the face sending me rolling on my side, stunned and ears ringing.

Knowing I needed to get off the floor quickly and jumping up, I just caught a glimpse out of the corner of my eye, the female was looking at something in her hand. Re-positioning it in her clenched fist, just as the male launched forward landing a kick to my thigh which made me curl over to the side a little, but still on my feet. At that very moment, the female moved in to attack me with her arm raised high in a stabbing manoeuvre.

I knew in that split second, I was in imminent danger, I couldn't see what was in her hand, whether it was a knife or a sharp. Hence, as she reached a position just above my head standing close enough to strike, I punched her with an uppercut to her jaw, which dropped her falling crashing into the upside-down table they had thrown.

The male then went berserk flying towards me with an all too common expression I have seen before, like a prison cell attack. After landing another blow to the side of my face, I felt comfortable bringing him down in a simple Tae kwon do movement quickly putting him down hard and with conviction on the carpet floor. The girl was conscious but moaning as she sat with her back to the wall, and the male was swearing at me telling me he was going to f****g kill me as I knelt on his back with his arm locked behind. At that point, another guard entered the room with a female store detective and took over from the arrest, whilst I asked Tanya on the ETA of the police and if she could check for me.

It all calmed down for the remaining fifteen minutes after with both the female and the male securely restrained but obviously still giving us the delight of their vocabulary.

The police arrived and placed them into silver and black bracelets, leading them out the door with the girl screaming she had been assaulted by me. A syringe with brown stuff half filling the tube was found with a one-inch needle exposed lying in the corner of the room where the girl fell. Handing this to the officer in a sharp's yellow safety bin, the officer said he would come back and take a statement from me in a short while as they left.

I had blank statements in my office, so after having a quick cigarette and coffee, I went ahead to write my witness statement for the police.

An hour and a half later, I had completed my statement in which time, the officer had rung to say that it will be tomorrow before he could return. These two had outstanding warrants of arrest, and the processing of them was delaying his return.

He briefly asked what had happened, and I told him the following: Male and female detained for trying to use a stolen credit card and showing abusive behaviour in-store. Credit card company confirmed it was stolen. When informing them, they were being detained; they both become violent and aggressive attacking me, throwing a table and two chairs at me. After being physically assaulted by both and witnessing what appeared to be a knife or a sharp, I used reasonable force to secure the situation in an attempt to prevent life-threatening injuries.

The officer said he would collect my statement tomorrow and not to worry about assault accusations. He added he was confident that when faced with the charges all adding up with existing outstanding offences, that the female would probably drop her accusation of an assault considering my statement.

He asked if I would like to press charges against them and I said no, I was just doing my job and that can be part of it, unfortunately.

Leaving the store, now nine o'clock, I was extremely late returning home and did not arrive until eleven-thirty, where I remember, sitting in the back garden having a cigarette thinking, "What a bloody day!"

Attempted Suicide

On the train to work this day was just like any other, but little did I know that today would see my life change forever. I remember with a clear head looking smart and fresh in my crisply ironed uniform and my highly polished boots. It was a bright sunny day as I walked through the city centre where people hurried to their place of work and to the city train station. The mood was good at my job with everyone in high spirits. Today we had three guards on duty and one store detective.

The day started with close observations of potential suspects which would not always manifest into any type of crime. There is not any single thing that can determine a criminal, just because they may look out of place in their appearance and their body language, does not always mean they are about to commit a crime.

It may be the case that there is an elegant, well-dressed individual, who looks like any respectable member of the public who is a prolific thief and is exceptionally good at it. Confidence seems to be a recipe for success and the smarter you may look, the less likely a camera or guard is to home in on you. This means that these calm individuals and masters of acting normal, achieve high theft counts and as such gain confidence about them that sends everyone off their scent. I have come across a few arrests where I have detained individuals like this, but you rarely catch them due to selection and concealment being their forte.

After lunch on this day around 2pm, I was called to the food floor, where a male was acting suspiciously in the alcohol aisle. He was an Afro Caribbean male of 5ft 10 inches, stockily built, scruffy black hair with a brown leather jacket on. Approaching the area, I called our CCTV room and asked Tanya to put the cameras on him, whilst I waited undetected on an adjacent aisle.

After five minutes Tanya radioed me to tell me she had observed selection of a bottle of whisky and he had it concealed within his leather jacket. He was now approaching the double glass doors that exited onto the car park at the back of the store. I asked for clarification that she had seen full selection, in clear view, with concealment and no attempt to replace the item back on the shelf. Tanya replied, "yes, it's all on tape in clear view, one hundred per cent confirmed the theft."

On hearing this and knowing Tanya's record of being an excellent CCTV operator, I made my way to the back doors, exiting ten feet behind him. He was walking with his left arm across his waist as he held the concealed bottle in his jacket. I approached him from his right side from behind, grabbing him by the wrist and his elbow.

I instructed him to calmly come back into the store as we have evidence that he has left the store with nonpayment for an item in his jacket.

At this point he said, "Yes Sir, I have, here is the bottle." passing me the bottle of whiskey which I took in my right hand, still holding his elbow with my left hand as I guided him back through the doors towards the escalator as we headed back to the holding room next to the CCTV room. On the long journey through three floors of shoppers, all looking at us as I escorted this detained male, I instantly felt sorry for him as he silently walked and climbed the escalators as it was almost like a long walk of shame. There was something about this male I could sense as he made his way into the holding room with his head held down in embarrassment and regret.

I asked him to sit down and instructed the two waiting security guards to keep an eye on him, whilst I talked to Tanya about the tape for evidence and if she had called the police and how long they would be. After ten minutes of collecting everything we needed for an open and shut case, I walked back into the holding room to see the two guards laughing and spraying deodorant into the room, where this male was. Quickly as I stepped in, I realised why they were doing this because the male had defecated and urinated himself.

Furious at their lack of humanity, I opened the door and told them both to f**k off out of this room before I threw them out, to which I had some evil looks of disapproval and some inappropriate comments as they left closing the door behind them. Disgusted with their behaviour, I apologised to the male, saying my name was Malcolm, and I will be processing him whilst I await the police officers to attend. I thought of taking him to the bathroom so he could become more comfortable. Still, there are all sorts of problems and rules that this breaks, even though it was clearly the kindest thing I could do, it was not allowed in any situation, so regretfully I had to wait for the police which caused me great sorrow to see a grown man in this situation.

I asked him his name as he sat with his head facing down looking at the floor, his legs and arms shaking. Then in triple speed, he stood to bolt upright, chest out, left arm by his side and right hand swung into a salute "25059…. Corporal Green Sir" he bellowed. My heart was feeling like a hot knife had been plunged deep into it as the seconds past, and my realisation overpowered my astonishment: He is one of my brothers—a fellow soldier. I asked him his first name, and he replied "Amos, Sir" I asked him to sit down and explain to me why he had stolen the whiskey.

His reply will live with me forever:

"Sir, Sir, please help me! I am homeless, I am an ex-soldier, I lost my family after I returned from Iraq." "I could not get the war out of my head, and I could not wash the blood off my hands." "My wife didn't understand and asked me to leave our home, I had no money, no family." "They stopped me seeing my children, and now I haven't seen them for 1 year." "I get attacked on the streets, pissed on, spat on, people are mean to me." "Doctors won't help me, and hospitals take me for a few days then I'm back on the streets." "People steal my money, I have no money for food, no family, and no home, please sir, help me, help me."

As Amos was talking to me, I was looking directly into his eyes as his body shook and his voice stuttered in desperation. His pupils were dark brown, almost black, the whites of his eyes, grey and bloodshot, the tears welled up in his sockets and his presence passing into my soul through this eye contact embraced my inner spirit. His cries for help were heartfelt and sincere, a spirit crying through the darkness in one last attempt for redemption. His sheer level of grief and trauma consumed me beyond any words.

I asked Amos, "why did you steal the whiskey?" He said, "for one last time," as he emptied eight bottles of paracetamol from his pockets. "Tonight, my pain will end." he said.

Standing up and stepping back in shock, I quickly glanced at him. Shaking, crying, and pleading for help, sitting in his own faeces with urine-soaked dirty black jeans, broken unbelievably, ridiculed, abused, assaulted, suffering from mental illnesses with deep routed trauma, forgotten and unloved.

My eyes had filled up with tears. My vision was now blurred with a tightening of my throat as I fought back the impulse to cry. My stomach was tensing, and a sick feeling came over me whilst an overwhelming sense of fear shuddered through my soul. His uncontrollable sobbing was heart-breaking to see. I was left speechless, with so much emotion going through my mind, mixed with anger and disgust.

Amos was still pleading with me, "please sir, help me, help me," as I continued silently to be drawn into his spirit through these eyes that could tell a thousand horror stories. I was utterly dumbfounded, like I was under the most powerful spell. Amos had rendered me with a broken heart and horrified to why humanity would allow this treatment and suffering of an ex-soldier who was once the reason why we all can sleep safely at night. His story was sinister and horrifying to hear as he appeared to me in the guise of a dark angel. Carrying a final warning on a personal level for my soul, which penetrated me to my very essence.

Just at that point, the police entered the room, two 6ft officers, with stocky build and radios echoing. "Hello, Amos." said one officer, "what have you been up to today?" "Theft of a bottle of whiskey," I answered. "Come on then Amos, you know the drill, let's get you back to the station, get you cleaned up and let's see if we can get a hot meal for you."

As Amos was leaving with his hands cuffed in front of him being guided out by the officer, with one hand holding his cuffs, he turned and looked at me once more as I made eye contact with him. That final stare took my breath away, and then Amos was gone.

Sitting down on the chair in the holding room, with the door closed in the musty smell that lingered and placing my head into my hands as I crouched for one moment, still in shock, with a sense that I had been given a warning from something higher than myself, I knew, my life would change from that day.

The journey home that day was sombre as I reflected on Amos and my own life.

That night I headed straight to the pub after quickly getting changed. It was Friday night, and I was determined to get smashed, not in a celebration way but in a morning kind of way, like at a wake. I felt a revelation that I knew was already rushing through my body, changing cellular structure. I felt something fantastic happening within me, like an awakening from a coma, and this feeling was something big.

Hugh came into the pub later, and I was pleased to see him as it had been ages since we had talked, albeit a little apprehensive. After a couple of pints, Hugh asked me to go with him. To venture off for another one of his dark evenings.

Quickly and with no hesitation, I said No, Hugh. That is not a life I choose for myself anymore. Laughing and saying, "you're alright, it will only be a quick run out." I continued to say, "No. Thank you, but No Hugh, I am done with that now, happy to have a beer with you, but that is it now." Extremely disappointed and continuing to try to persuade me, Hugh finally red-faced, decided to leave. It got a little sensitive there for a moment as I could see he was deeply offended and I did like Hugh, but I was clear and very sure that from today my life would change and tomorrow would mark that change in an even bigger way.

I knew, there was only one route for me now to take, and that was education. Education would open doors to me that have been previously closed, it would give me a focus and a purpose in life. I got to work investigating suitable courses, downloaded applications, and eagerly filled them out.

By the end of the weekend, I had sent off my application request for University to enrol in a BSc Hons Sport and Exercise Nutrition Degree. Hoping my culinary background and qualifications as a chef would meet the credits needed to get accepted. I also sent off my student loan application and supporting letters. I really did feel like an angel had touched my heart.

Machete Man

Travelling to work on the train seemed to be a new experience for me as I somehow looked at people differently now. Curious, what drama the other people were experiencing in their lives as I people watched from my window seat. Looking at their facial expressions, body language, and behaviour. There seemed to be more miserable people than there was happy for sure.

My approach and attitude had changed too, not so forceful, but relatively calm, collective, and professional.

I had already made up my mind, my time was nearing the end. I no longer looked at the criminals with hatred and disgust, instead of curiosity, wondering what situation in their life is propelling them towards crime and how utterly desperate and lost they must be feeling.

After detaining three individuals for petty theft in the morning, I had taken my lunch break, which was interrupted by an emergency call from Tanya to evacuate the building. After some quick communication, I was horrified to hear the reason why. There was a six-foot-four Afro-Caribbean male in the lingerie section with a machete, and customers were fleeing the store in a panic. Entering the area near the department, I reached for my radio." "Charley, one approaching the second floor by the escalator, put the cameras on me as I am about to approach the male." Turning my radio to the almost off position as the radio went crazy with voices in a disapproval manner from all routes, I approached the male.

Slowly getting about eight foot away from him with both hands raised in the surrender mode, he was wearing a long dark jacket down to his knees and had long black dreadlocks. He was a large stature and looked like he was heavily medicated or on drugs. As I slowly stepped closer, asking him to stay calm and tell me his name. He looked at me speechless.

I told him that there were people frightened in the lingerie section that needed to exit the store and that I wanted him to slowly put the machete on the floor and step away from it. I told him I meant him no harm and that if he put this weapon down, he could leave the store through the exit behind him, which lead to the second floor of the shopping centre.

To my amazement, he did follow my instructions, placing down the machete, standing upright, looking at me once more and turning to leave slowly towards the exit. Currently, the three ladies were hurrying toward the escalator clearly distressed and making their way towards the front entrance of the store. I gave a big sigh of relief as I looked at the weapon on the floor whilst turning up my radio and calling all call signs that the male was no longer in my store and had entered the shopping centre unarmed as I had the machete.

Now it would appear, he was no immediate threat to the public, but he still needed apprehending by the police, asking the CCTV room to monitor his movements until he could be detained.

Back in the CCTV room, Tanya was furious and was not prepared to listen to my explanation of my actions. I tried to explain that elderly women were in imminent danger and after an uncomfortable heated five-minute discussion, I told Tanya that I resign as head guard effective immediately.

Surprisingly, this stopped her in her tracks. She became silent as I handed her my radio and ID card.

Walking past dumbstruck guards and exiting the CCTV room immediately and making my way to the escalator's whilst throwing on my jacket, taking a last look at the store, as I walked towards the front door, leaving and not looking back. Lighting a cigarette as if it were a fat Cuban cigar, making my way through the city center.

Very shortly, I was on the train pulling out of Birmingham New Street with a satisfying relief, that I would never work in security again.

Dissecting Human Brains

After several days of going fishing a realigning my spirit with nature, I received the news I was praying for. I had received an offer of a place at University.

Meeting up with Jim in a pub in town, I told him that I was starting University on a BSc Hons Sport and Exercise Nutrition Degree. Turning his head and looking at me with his wide-eyed shock face, he paused and swallowed before starting to laugh, "are you sure." "Yes," I said, "I have got a place, if I can become a soldier, I can become anything." Jim giggled and said, "well done, you, go for it."

He knew what I did not and was probably thinking I had no idea what I was letting myself in for.

Going to University at the age of thirty-two after secretly weeks before being addicted to crack cocaine was a massive shock. Sure, my classmates were all accepting of me, and I made many good friends, and we attended many great nights out together, but I was totally out of my depth. It had been 17 years since I had sat in a classroom, and my forte then was fighting, not study. So, I thought I would have to approach this in steps and purchased the study skills learning book, which basically helps you get organized. The second was to buy all my academic module books for each lesson, that was achievable with my student loan. Next was to Dictaphone each lesson to replay it at home, while I studied the subject. Getting in front of myself to study up on the readings for the following morning helped immensely too. Partnering up with a smart girl called Jane, helped my practical laboratory lessons, all with a sheer determination to get through one day at a time the best way I could. I also purchased the power of intention by Dr W Dyre, which gave me strength and belief in my inner abilities.

Completing the first year and surprisingly achieving honours in Anatomy and Physiology, I decided that I would prefer to transfer to the pathology degree as I seemed to have a natural blending with this subject area and so I applied.

I had achieved enough academic points to transfer, and the following term, I would start another three years on the BSc (Hons) Biomedical Science co-terminus degree. This excited me, and I was crazy about it.

Studying until 4am in the morning often. Going to my local began to be outdated. Of course, everyone laughed at me in the pub when I told them what I was doing. Absolutely no one believed that I could do a degree, apart from perhaps, my wife.

After the first year, I was disappointed with my grades, but I struggled on the computer in all fairness. I had to learn from scratch how to use one. It was challenging and emotionally draining at times. I recall crying on the train home more than once due to the pressure and deadlines. Still, after some time, I was offered a placement at the Princess Royal Hospital in Telford and the Royal Shrewsbury Hospital, where I would attempt to complete a pathology state registration portfolio.

I rotated through many disciplines, such as Hematology, Microbiology, Bronchoscopy, Colposcopy, Biochemistry, Histology, Cytology, and Breast Clinic. Culminating in completing my final year and passing my state registration portfolio with the Health Professions Council in Microbiology.

In the final year, my wife and I ended our marriage, selling our home, and after leaving half for her and buying her a new car for my children, I moved into student halls at the University.

This was an awful experience; living with eighteen-year-olds trashing the communal kitchen was hard to bear. I stuck it out and started to apply for positions within Biomedical Science.

With money from my half of the house sale, I went down to London and had my teeth smartened up, so I had a friendly American style smile, and I had bought some nice suits which complemented with my designer shoes and Armani glasses, I looked great and felt great.

I purchased a Volvo S80 executive flying machine, which complemented the transformation I was trying to achieve. This emanated my confidence, and after two interviews, I had received an offer as a Biomedical Scientist in Microbiology in Bristol. Surprisingly also a phone call from The John Radcliffe Hospital in Oxford within Neuro and Ocular Pathology. The telephone call said that the position had been filled. Still, as the laboratory manager, she was so impressed by my interview, she had applied to create a post for me as a Biomedical scientist state registered.

I could not believe this phone call, not only was this hospital one of the top training hospitals in the country, but they were so impressed with me they had created a new position just for me! I was floating on clouds.

The John Radcliffe was a fantastic opportunity, and the hospital was a world player in Cancer biology partnered with Oxford Universities Division of Neuroscience. After little consideration, I chose to accept the offer at the John Radcliffe Hospital, and I soon I would start my first role as a Biomedical Scientist in Neuropathology.

In four short years, I had gone from being a security guard running after criminals on minimum wage to being a state registered Biomedical Scientist working with and alongside Oxford Universities Division of Neuroscience. Every day was like living a dream, I had my own private suite with a private bathroom, an executive car, and a 34k salary which after receiving many pay scale rises ended up at 38k.

I was single, and life couldn't be better. My role within the laboratory had many directions, from slide preparation, microtome work, and preparation of cases for coroner's court. We also worked heavily in tumour diagnostics, brain dissection, and emergency fine needle biopsies. These were taken in open brain surgery operations daily. The surgeon would take a patient into the operating theatre, locate the tumour, and take a fine needle biopsy. He would then send it to me, and I would do a series of tests, including stains, where I would diagnose and name the tumour within fifteen minutes. Informing the surgeon of the tumour grade, type, and information on whether it was a primary tumour or secondary, benign, or metastatic, all by microscopic investigations.

If the tumour had breast tissue cells and was taken from the brain, I knew it had passed the lymph nodes and was a malignant secondary tumour.

I thoroughly enjoyed working as a Biomedical Scientist, and my laboratory manager Hillary Brown, was always fantastic, professional, and I would like to think, almost my friend. She was kind and thoughtful, understanding, and a great teacher.

I admired her calm and professional teaching skills, and on a personal level, she was a lovely, intelligent woman. Dr Wayne Squires was also a lovely lady and incredibly smart being one of the world's experts in shaken baby syndrome. I worked closely with Dr Wayne and recall throwing a staff Christmas buffet at her home where my favourite helper Jim, came to assist. That was an exciting night.

After some time, I had gained competence, and I was often left to close the lab down and stand by for any emergency biopsy tests. Working with world-renowned consultants like Dr Margarette Esri, Dr Wayne Squires, and Dr Olaf, allowed my professional inclusion into some of the highest regarded diagnostic practices which were then lectured and taught to Oxford University students.

One of my weekly roles was to demonstrate brain dissection to the MSc students at Oxford University with Dr Wayne Squires. Also assisting her in forensic pathology of pediatric neuropathology investigations for the high court in suspicious infant deaths.

As the years moved forward, I thoroughly enjoying my Oxford journey becoming academically close to my Specialist Biomedical Scientist title and my fourth pay rise, when I decided to change my direction in life. My day would often be spent documenting child deaths, terminally ill records and collecting brain and tissue samples from the morgue. I would almost every day see dead children. This was just a constant reminder of how much I missed my own children, and I had to be honest with my own pursuit of happiness and wellbeing.

It was a privilege and an honour to work with some of the most intelligent people in the world and be the holder of the title Biomedical scientist and be classed, recognized, professionally and academically as one of them.

I had a strong calling to become a religious priest, where I could help and guide individuals, especially if they found themselves lost in life. I had gained the belief that life was about choices. I felt that I had walked enough in the darkness slowly crawling to the light that I could also reach out my hand to other spirits that may be lost, needing help finding their way home.

Walking the path of a religious priest was deeply spiritual which opened my eyes to kindness, compassion, and love. Seeing things, I never knew existed and experiencing the true power of love.

I enjoyed this challenge immensely, and I had the pleasure of helping many people over the next six years, achieve in life, what many people said they could not.

Helping people take just one more step, every day, in the direction of light and hope, leaving sadness, pain and regret in the past gave me an overwhelming purpose in life which I still practice and enjoy to this day.

"I know you will find this true story filled with hidden life meanings and lessons. I have been entirely transparent within this book in the hope that you may too, find the courage to make the right choices in life, remembering nothing is out of your reach, no matter how far down the well you are."

"Thank you for sharing this journey with me and for holding my hand until the end."

"May you be blessed with love, light, and safety."

Love Malc xx

Printed in Great Britain
by Amazon

46429593R00132